Dear

Basquiat:

A Letter to

My Black Son

Peter R. Dowdy

Dope Art Dealers Houston

A Dope Art Dealers Book

Published by Dope Art Books

Copyright 2019 by The Union, Co.

For information address: Dope Art Dealers Books

ISBN # 9781081027179

Published in the United States of America

For my son, Basquiat

And every other

father and son in the world.

Contents

Acknowledgements

It's probably someone I will forget to thank so I'll first sum up to thanking everyone that I have encountered throughout my whole life. From the doctor helping my mother give birth to me to the cashier who gave me my receipt yesterday, thank you all.

A special thanks goes to my mother and father for raising me. You've done your best and this is the outcome. You can at least say you raised a talented author, artist, producer, entrepreneur and father to your list of accomplishments. You've done well. It wasn't always peaches and cream but peanut butter and jelly would be the best descriptive combo to explain my childhood. I thank you for that and I love you both dearly.

To my wife, thank you for responding in the DMs. I have art because of you. I have love because of you. I have hope because of you. Thank you for everything.

To my best friend Kris, thanks for being the brother I never had. I could have lost my life in many ways but you've made sure to live your purpose and help me every time. Can't thank you enough.

To all my friends, associates, co-workers, crew members, thank you for giving me hope in knowing that I would be successful. Your dreams for me to make it big is an inspiration alone that is unexpected yet appreciated dearly. I will remember each and every single one of you all always.

To my past lovers, thank you for the experience of knowledge gained through our relationships. I've learned from each of you one way or another that makes me into the man I am now. I apologize for any pain felt and its effects and I pray that you all are in a better space now than you were with me.

To my siblings Kristen, Cece and Michelle (RIP), thank you for being an awesome group of Black women that I look up to. Not only because you all are older than me, but because we've all had our similar struggles but different paths. I'm proud nonetheless of all of you and the women and mothers you have become today. I know you're looking down on me Michelle and you're proud of your baby bro. Keep shining!

To my extended family, my Aunts, Uncles, cousins, nephews, nieces, in-laws, I thank you all for your love and support of me in the past years. I know me being an author is surprising to most of you but I'm sure you're all proud of me and what I have accomplished thus far. You all have been a light in my path in some sort, so I thank you all from the bottom of my heart.

Dear Basquiat

To my dear, sweet angel of a child, the first thing I want to say is that I love you.

Secondly, I want to let you know that I apologize for how your future may be. I apologize for the awkwardness I bring to the family. I apologize for the hope that we'd be best friends forever. I apologize for all the terrible jokes you're going to hear.

I apologize for being an influence on your behavior in your life, for any missed opportunities I wasn't there for, for not being strong enough, for not being smart enough and for simply not teaching you something you felt I should have along the way. Please forgive me for it all.

I'm learning the best way I know how and this book will give you the background for my knowledge in hopes that you would understand how and why I am the way that I am; bringing better knowledge into who you really are. You're the most amazing thing that has ever happened to me! So much better looking as a baby, I can only imagine the looks you'll get when you get older. You're just so handsome. You're perfect in so many ways and your laugh is so…heartwarming.

This is my ode to you. I owe you more than you know and I just want you to grow knowing that I am not perfect (although at times I may seem like I am).

I have my flaws, Lord, do I have my flaws!

I have my doubts, my weaknesses, my habits, my insecurities and all. But I have you. I have hope that my goals, my dreams, my aspirations, my love will NEVER fail because of you.

You inspire me to do better. You are an inspiration for my steadfastness, my defeat with procrastination, my comfort to a long day, my reason for tears of joy, my smile when one isn't present. You're the reason for a lot of things. Never the blame, but you're just a reason. You're a beautiful reason.

I'm grateful for having the opportunity to show you the way of life and the chance to be the best guide I can be. Just know...the road map I have was on clearance so you know I had to get that because your Dad is cheap so I'm doing the best I can.

I also apologize if answers come in the form of no and it hurts. I'm coming from a good place most of the time and know that life is full of no's, but you're going to have to push through all of them to get to the yes that life feels you deserve. Create your own yes. I'm here to help, and yes you have one of the most frugal parents ever to fund all your needs, but I will make sure that every single one of them is met.

Why?

Because you deserve better than I had.

You're better than me and if ever it seems like I'm hard on you, I apologize ahead of time. This is all I know. This world can be crazy for you and I and I'm not sure of what the future holds for you, but it's yours for the taking. I'm just here to make sure you can handle it all. I love you like you'll never know, but hopefully this book will bring you closer knowing just how much I do.

So, About These Farts

Yeah, hi! It's Daddy here! Some refer to me as Peter (government name). Some refer to me as Shawn. Some refer to me as Krow. Why different names, you'll find out later. But to you, I'm Dad. It takes a bit of comfort for me to ALLOW people to call me by my government name. Just know, you will NEVER have that comfort! Just stick to Dad or Daddy and we'll be fine.

What are you like almost 11 months now?

I've had a pretty interesting life up to your arrival and surprisingly I've managed to keep that interest up afterwards. There's a lot to know about your Dad. In fact, I'm not even around you right now. Don't worry; I'm not in prison (although as you read you'll be surprised I'm not).

I'm actually working here in Alaska for a few months to save up some money to do more things with businesses that your mother and I have. We're looking to get a house soon when I return so you can have a yard to play in and we don't have to live in anymore apartments (Ownership! We'll get to that later).

But more about me, I think I'm funny because I make myself laugh as well as others. I've been pretty good at making you chuckle a time or two so don't try to play me like I'm not.

Sometimes I pick my boogers and eat them when no one is around (especially the thick dry ones...just something about those...but never the snot...that's just gross).

Sometimes I smoke marijuana, which you'll learn as you get older has been a constant move on towards getting legal everywhere throughout the US. Right now it's not legal in Texas so your Dad's kind of a rebel.

Sometimes I laugh when people fall down stairs or slip on a wet surface.

Sometimes I work a job long enough to get paid for training and then I quit. It's long enough to learn about a job and early enough to stop before doing it longer than you need.

Sometimes I eat cookie dough before the cookies even make it into the oven. The package says don't but you know me, rebel. Plus I've been doing this for years, if I were to get salmonella, I should have had it by now at least once.

Sometimes I've peed in the bed well over my twenties which I'll also suggest if you're going to do a water based diet, make sure to use the restroom before you go to sleep. Oh and make sure to pee before lying down if you've been drinking. Save yourself the troubles. If you're lazy like me at times, lying in wet sheets in the bed because you don't want to get up is for the birds. Do better.

Sometimes I fart. I fart by myself. I fart in crowds. I fart at church. I fart at parties. I just fart. I'm the type that can't really hold it in because it hurts more to keep it in than it does releasing it. I know that's something you probably don't want to hear about but... yeah. You started reading a chapter called "So About These Farts", you should've prepared yourself my boy. But anyways, this is your Dad. I've been a pretty gassy guy for as long as I remember. I'm not lactose intolerant or anything. I just have gas. Oh and I take a LOT of shits, yes, shits. It's a word like "hippopotamus" and "pickles". It's not a bad word unless you make it bad (don't tell your mother I said that though). Sometimes the shit comes when you only think it's a fart but it's really like a bonus feature like when Lil Wayne comes on a remix verse after like 6 other rappers. The fart is more like the instrumental and boy do my farts have bass.

From the thought of it, I think you may be blessed with the same instrument. At least that's what your diapers are telling me. It's funky like the 70s.

But it's something you should know about farts. Farts are something that everyone does but are ashamed of doing in public with anyone knowing when, kind of like voting. It's weird. But it's just like that. Some people fart and don't say anything and let the smell linger into the air laying the smack down on any candy ass's nostril.

Then they're those assholes (pun intended) who blame someone else for their fart because they're THAT embarrassed. Can you believe that? That's like if you sneezed and the mist is just floating in the air and someone turns around thinking it's you but you play it off by rubbing your nose while nonchalantly pointing in someone else's direction. (Sidebar: That's very disgusting by the way, please don't be that type of person; just cover your mouth at ALL TIMES when sneezing).

But yeah, it's like that, I'm like "Who raised you?"

It's going to be some times in life where you do something where others may find it odd or whatever and it's okay. They may say whatever they feel like, which everyone is entitled to their opinion. But a great saying goes, "Assholes are like opinions. Everyone has one." Remember that one. It will take you a looooong way my child. But those are just going to be opinions. That's all. You'll have to learn to let it go. Like a fart. Fuck holding that shit in. Release! Drop that album. But…(pun intended again), just make sure you say excuse me. It's like a code word for "my bad" or "I apologize for the funk you are about to witness". Trust me, just say it. It tends to make the opinions back off a bit.

Now there have been instances where my farts have gotten me in good situations and bad at the same time. One in particular I remember was in middle school. I had to be in like 6th grade or something. But I remember I had to have had one too many Oreos the night before and my digestive system was going to make sure I got the memo.

So I'm sitting in class, taking a test. And although you're too young to know what that is right now, you'll know it's just one of the times in class when it's the quietest. You can hear a pin drop. You can hear the birds outside a room with no windows saying "Arrr…that kid looks like he has gas….arrrr" How did they know? Crows are very smart birds but they'll snitch on you in a minute.

But here I am in class at test time. In school back then if you wanted to get a girl's attention, you had to get a reason to go to the front of the class so she can see you and your fly ass outfit. Fubu was the shit back then. If you're wearing that now by the time you're old enough to read this, I'll be thoroughly impressed.

But in my class was Marcella, skinny bright skinned girl with glasses. She was so pretty and not many boys liked girls with glasses cause they were considered nerds or girls that weren't "fast". You'll learn that term "fast" later, but know she just wasn't. But that's what I liked. I liked the girls that no one else liked. Some call it bad taste, I call it my own lane. You will get to determine your own lane when you're older son. I promise you that.

So with the pencil sharpener being across the front of the class, that gave me a reason to get up so I could be seen. I broke my pencil on purpose so I could make sure I'm at the pencil sharpener longer to get a good sharpen and to give her a good look. I took as long as I could and looked around the room in her direction and she looked back.

My plan worked! Yes!

Little did I know there was another plan I wasn't aware of.

It was Plan F.

I thought I was going to be fly and walk past her desk to ask the teacher about a question on the test. Haha! Boy was I wrong. I walked towards her and I let out a fart but this one was silent. No sound, no nothing. I was semi safe. No one knew if they smelled it. Maybe. Maybe I was nervous or maybe it was those damn cookies.

I just knew, something was about to go down.

After speaking to the teacher at their desk, I got that "bubble". And son, if you ever get that "bubble", don't try to hold it in. Just remember farts can be like balloons; the longer you hold the bubble, the louder the pop. Let's just say I made myself the clown at the birthday party that day. When I sat back at my desk (which weren't ordinary chairs, these were hard echoes we happen to sit on), that bubble popped. Not like a pop like the gun before the horses run in a race, I mean that bubble turned into Louis Armstrong himself and made a symphony sound like a whistle.

If I ever wanted her attention, I got it for sure right then! The whole class was laughing at me. Did I feel embarrassed? No. I did that shit. It was no denying it. No pointing at any one else. It was me. Everyone knew.

The laughs were going on for a bit longer than needed to the point the teacher had to calm down the class. Funny thing is, no one really even knew my name before I farted. No one did except the teacher. After that, I was known. I was somebody. Yes, I was the kid that farted. But you knew me. And I had the power to give people the joy of laughter without trying. Everyone could have easily been like "Eww... you nasty" or even worse, the infamous "scoot over" technique, which is a highly contagious move for others. You never want to be the one people scoot away from, EVER! But it didn't happen that way. I just shrugged off the incident because knowing me, it was bound to happen again, possibly the next class. But Marcella knew my name, and what could have been embarrassment turned into opportunity.

So yes farting is normal. It can have its good and bad. But it's natural. So is the feeling of being embarrassed. But things happen all the time you're not ready for and we can either be embarrassed about the things that happen to us or we can own that shit (pun not intended) and move on.

But let that fart be a representation of your personality. Don't hold it in. Let it out. Do you and be you. You'll thank yourself sooner or later for the opportunities that come out of it. Let the world smell who you are. Forget who doesn't like it, because you're not living your life for the comfort of others. You're living your life for you. Stay gassy San Diego. (That's a Ron Burgundy reference, you might understand it later). And remember, say excuse me. That's really important.

Oh God, I Already Know

So this chapter isn't one to tell you I know everything or to tell you that you're wrong, this is just one to simply tell you I am aware of a lot and that I'm not wrong. Let me tell you that you're my son, no doubt about that. I didn't even get a paternity test because you were born looking just like me in a way. I always thought that there was no way a baby could be born looking like an adult male, until you were born. During your mother's pregnancy I had my doubts. She can't tell you that because there was no way I was going to ask your mom "How do I know it's mine"?

NO WAY!

For one, she's too sweet of a woman to hurt her feelings in that manner. Never hurt a sweet woman. Karma is your auntie and she only shows up to teach you a hard lesson. Those are one of those times. Trust me, you don't want her to show you that lesson. I learned too many times. Two, I just trusted her. She's never given me a reason to NOT trust her. She's fucking wonderful and I'm lucky to even still have her.

Three, there was no way in the world you could explain to a woman a man's doubt when it comes to pregnancy. I had to ask God to give me guidance, strength and knowledge. No, God isn't the neighbor next door. God is the one who obviously trusted me to be your father and your mother to be your mom. Who is God? Eh, who really knows. A lot of people question so much about who God really is. Some think it's a man. Some think it's a woman. Some think it's a holy spirit in the sky. Some don't think God exists at all. Although I can't exactly feel comfortable in teaching you what I was taught about who God is because of my ignorance and confusion. I'll tell you who God is to me. So I'll just start by sharing this with you. I'll just skip the birds and the bees context and just let you know straight up, me and your mother had sex. PLENTY OF SEX! So much sex that you could have had so many brothers and sisters if it weren't for hot towels to wipe them on and Taco Bell napkins when we couldn't find those hot towels. But when a man and a woman have sex, they can potentially create something like a baby or a disease, or both. We got lucky and just had you.

To be honest, you could have been born earlier but we had a miscarriage months before we found out we were having you for real. That was a hard time for both your mother and I. Nonetheless, I made sure I stayed by her side through it all because that's just what a real man does. NEVER leave a woman to be by her lonesome; especially if you played a part in the situation that she's in. NEVER! So after the miscarriage, your mom and I moved in together in our first apartment. It was all new to us. This was my first time getting an apartment that didn't involve me staying on someone's couch (that someone being your Uncle Kris). I felt like a man. I was paying bills and taking care of someone I loved so much. I've waited for this for a long while. That feeling. Then Harvey happened. I know what you're thinking.

Who's Harvey? What did he do?

Did he have sex with mom? Did he hurt mom?

No son. He fucked us both!

I guess this would be a perfect time to let you know that Harvey isn't a guy (you'll learn about personification and sarcasm later in life, this I know). Harvey was the hurricane that came through Houston where we stayed in August of 2017. Harvey fucked us good. Good and raw. Crazy thing is, we lost our car three weeks before Harvey even came during a flood that got water all in our car. So by the time the hurricane hit, we were already in a rental with one week left on it. The hurricane flooded our apartment the hell out! I know, why didn't we stay on the second floor or third floor? Why would you get an apartment on the first floor? Look son, you're going to find out a lot of things on your own in life. But like I said before, my job is to let you learn the opposite of the hard way. We got the first floor apartment because it was cheap. Everything was cheap in the Greenspoint area. It was hella convenient for us both because we had furniture we wanted to move in soon. I mean we just got our first bed together not even weeks before the hurricane. Me and your mom had our shit together. Then pow! Harvey hit and changed a lot. We were homeless. We were a couple in love only together for like five months; homeless, but together. We stayed in a shelter for like a week. Just your mom, your brother BJ and myself, on our own. Then we stayed at my sister's apartment while she was gone out of town being a flight attendant for like a week. We stayed with my parents for like a week or two and that didn't work out with my dad being the way he can be (I'll explain later) and then we moved in with your mom's parents (which wasn't the best situation but it was a situation we could deal with until we got our own place again).

It took about a month after that and we finally got our own apartment again. Yes son, not on the first floor. We were on the third this time. I learned my lesson. Shut up. Now, here she was in October and telling me she's pregnant, again! My insecurities were out of this world! Like how could a woman love me so much to stick with me through thick and thin and still want to be with me through it all? How could she be so faithful to a guy like me? I mean, I was faithful too. But my past wasn't exactly spotless you know? Neither was hers but we were okay with that because we were good to each other. Had respect for one another and listened to what each other's needs were and tried our best to cater to that. But me though? How was I this blessed to have such a sweetheart? Someone so loving that would trust me to be a great father to our baby. I think every guy questions "But is it mine?" in the midst of so many insecurities. But like I said, I wasn't going to ask her that. Deep down inside I felt you were mine. I just knew it. If the trust was there, and she was there through all of that turmoil months before and still stuck around my silly ass. Of course you're mine. I KNOW!

How do I know? Because God answered my prayer.

I asked for guidance, strength and knowledge. Remember that? I didn't know what to do when I first found out your mom was pregnant the first time. I just knew to be there. And with all that went on, good and bad, your mom and I were guided in the right direction at ALL times. I wasn't strong enough to take care of myself before I met your mom, but all of the sudden meeting her was all the strength I needed to keep pushing. And knowledge, shiiiiiiit... let your mom tell it to everyone else, I don't know shit. But when we're alone, she talks to me sweet and lets me know that that I know just what to do and when to do it. Let me tell it, I just say, thanks God for that knowledge you somehow gave to me and not to my wife because she STILL thinks I know what I'm doing. But between you and me son, I don't. I really don't. But neither do you, and that's the beauty of continuous learning. You never know all the answers to everything, but you can always find out. And parents always find out! ALWAYS! I used to think I could get away with murder (not that I've murdered anyone, somehow your mom thinks differently). I'll tell you this other story which is a hard lesson.

Remember I told you about your Aunt Karma? Okay so, I feel it's right for you to know who your Dad really is, dirty past and all. So growing up I used to be a kleptomaniac. No that's not some cool ass name for a crazy robot. Your Dad used to steal, I mean a lot! When I think of the reason why I believe it's mainly because I didn't like to hear no, which I heard almost ALL the time when I asked for something growing up. I took it upon myself to get it myself without having to ask. I can almost guarantee you every time I went to the story with your Mimi (my mom), I stole SOMETHING! We'd be at Walmart and she'd be shopping and I would tell her I'm going to the bathroom or something and I would go steal something like a super size pack of batteries for my Game Boy Color (if you're reading this too mom, yeah I did it... sorry). Or when I thought that was old, I graduated to stealing CDs.

Huh? What you mean what are CDs?

Boy are you listening? I don't have time to explain what types of things music was played on right now. Just know I was stealing and this wasn't a good thing. I thought I was getting away with it. Years went by and I just kept stealing for no reason. Sometimes the gifts for Christmas I got my family were stolen. I just wanted them to be happy and show them I appreciated them for what they've done for me. Yeah it was a real fucked up way to show them. But I had to do something for them. That's what families do, no matter what. I'm not telling you to start stealing at all. Matter of fact, just don't! If you ever feel the need to where you even have to steal, please ask me. If I say no, don't go stealing it. I know that's what you'll think. And don't tell me "But if you say no, I might steal it". I know you'll probably find some way to blackmail me into getting what you want so let's just cut the shit right now. I love you and I'll get you what you need. But for the love of God, please never ask me for Jordans. My parents never got me a pair, not because they couldn't afford it (they wouldn't afford it, there's a difference) but because it symbolized something I knew I never needed. Material things are just that, material.

Nothing to ever be so attached to or something we feel we must get by any means, even by stealing it. White people did that to get America. Would you want someone you don't know to come into our house and take your toys and say they found them and they're theirs? I know. Didn't think so. That's American History for you in a nutshell. Happy 4th of July.

But yeah so, high school comes. It's my senior year. I haven't gotten into trouble all year until February comes. One day, I'm staying after school walking around chilling because I don't want to come home early. Most likely IF my Dad was home, he was going to make me do some chores I didn't want to do or something like that. I wasn't having it that day. So yep, after school it was. I was walking around and walked past the gymnasium and what do I see? A gym floor full of purses everywhere! I walked in and shouted, "Hello! Is it me you're searching for?" (that was a Lionel Richie insert, I know you don't know nothing about that). No one responded. So I took it upon myself to grab the most expensive purse I could, stuffed it under my tall tee shirt (tall tees are something I'll explain more later… it's embarrassing) and I took off. Went to the restroom around the corner, looked through the purse and found only $13 and a bunch of jewelry, keys, credit cards (which I'm wondering what kind of white girl has a credit…never mind) and other useless things. I took the money of course and left everything else in the purse. Now at this time, I got what I wanted. Money. That's what I expected to be in the purse. Wouldn't you? Of course you would. I know. But something in me didn't want to be the only one to benefit from my mischief. I'll tell you right now before going any further... if and again I'm not condoning you in anyway to steal, but if you so ever feel to take it upon yourself to do so, never and I mean NEVER EVER involve anyone else in your wrongdoing. It can save you a lot of headache, time and pain (and to be honest it can also help you not get caught... wink). But I involved my friends that day. I took the purse to them after meeting them in the cafeteria and showed them the purse. They went through it like some damn savages! I don't know who all took what, but I do know this one girl took the girl who owned the purse's class ring that was in it. How did you know you ask? Good question. I knew you would ask that.

The next day, I get called in the office during third period and I see old girl who took the ring in the office (mind you at the time I didn't know she had it). I stayed in trouble so I didn't really think too much of her being in there but as SOON as I walk in I ask her what she was doing in there. She's going to say out loud "Man they got us!" Inside my head I'm like "Biiiiiiiiiiiiiiiiiiiiiitch whatchu mean they got US?" Instantly I knew, they knew. So to make this long story short, they caught me cause the girl who took the ring wore it in one of her classes. Guess who was in that class? Damn boy! You good! Of course, the girl who the purse belongs to. That big dummy! See, this is the MAIN reason why I say never involve others in your mischief. Their sloppiness and carelessness can get you in deeper trouble itself. It's best not to do bad all in all. But definitely not with others. EVER! I got in-school suspension for the rest of the year because of that incident. The girl's parents decided not to press charges, which saved me a lot as far as the future goes. But I wasn't allowed to go to prom nor stay after school anymore. They were not going to let me graduate, but my mom wasn't having that. I told her I didn't do it, and I don't think she believed me, but she said she did (if you're still reading Mom, sorry, I did that too) Your grandma is a rider. Not in the way your mom is. Your grandma is the lady who came up to the elementary school and showed her presence when they told her I threw poop on the kid in the next stall in 1st grade. I did that shit. The same lady who showed up to school when they told her I peed on the kid in the restroom in 5th grade. I did that shit too. But not your mom.

Your mom is probably going to let me go down for something like that because she's not going to want to be involved in something so negative. But that's the good in your mom. Balance. She'll ride for something positive. That's what I

29

needed in my life, someone to keep my head straight and stay on the straight and narrow. A positive path in life you could say. I owe my mother and your mother a lot. But that was your Aunt Karma showing her ass, teaching me a hard lesson that life is sure to give you whatever you think you're getting away with doing something wrong. So whenever you think you're getting away with something, just know that you're my son, and I already know. That's that knowledge I asked God for still at work…wink again.

But This Is Our Love

Want to hear about the story of how me and your mom met? Of course you do. And I promise it's a lot cleaner than how you were born. First let me tell you a little more about who I am so you know exactly who your mom chose to say yes to. This might make the clarity of who your parents really are a little clearer. Your Dad is the type of guy that has had the history of having his heart broken and breaking hearts as well. I've had my share of "You ain't shits" and "You'll never find a woman like me again". If you're anything like me, you will have yours too. But let's not make that a goal. Let's be better than Dad.

Can we agree on that?

What do you mean you're way ahead of me? Whatever!

Okay so backtrack to my first heart break. This shit was the worst and it kind of sets a tone to my thought process on a lot of other things like religion, long distance, what love really is, kids, the whole nine. I was dating this girl back in high school. I was on the Northwest side of Houston, she was on the Southwest. If you're even slightly more knowledgeable of Houston and its traffic and roads than your mother is, you can understand like most Houstonians, Houston is really an hour away from Houston. Back then in like 2005, Houston seemed a lot bigger than it was for most. Especially for teenagers without cars. Google wasn't really popping like that back then. Imagine that! How did we get from one place to another? We had Map Quest. It was like Google Maps but watered down. If you didn't have a GPS, you had to print out your destination to where you were going and actually FOLLOW directions.

Make a slight left here.

Go down 3 miles.

Turn left onto 290.

Stay on 290 for 3 days.

Then make a slight right onto I-10.

Stay on I-10 for 2 weeks.

You will arrive next year.

Very complex and basic. Plus, it had to be harder for you to read print outs while you drive to get to somewhere in your own city. But this was our life. Thank God for Google (someone else had to ask for that knowledge too). But this girl across town was special to me. She had my heart at the time. Dark skinned ghetto queen, she was mine, all mine. Until... one day I'm at church sitting in the back and I get a text on my phone. It reads "We need to talk". Now son, I wouldn't be doing you my duty of a father if I didn't give you the heads up on the "We need to talk" text. There are only two reasons you'll ever get that message. Either you fucked up or she fucked up. There's no in between. So WHENEVER you get that text, don't respond right away. Just take a minute to think about anything you may have done wrong. Take an hour if need be, we're men (well you will be), we might need that long. If in that hour you realize that you're in the clear of any wrong doing, just take another moment before responding. I didn't do that.

I rushed in because I was so anxious as to find out what she needed to talk about. So I texted back almost immediately like a dumbass, "What's wrong babe, what you need to talk about?" or some silly shit like that. She texted back minutes later, "Are you at home?" I responded no. She then sent, "Call me when you get home so we can talk." I had

33

NO idea of what this conversation could be like. I was 17 and hella naïve. I was super clueless. I wished someone put me up on game for what transpired afterwards. So I get home, rush out of my church clothes and went to call her outside because I felt it was important and a serious conversation at least enough to not let others over hear what was being said. I called and she told me first "Promise me you won't be mad". Now son, this is another fair warning. If a woman ever tells you to promise you won't be mad by her telling you something, she legit knows you have the potential to kill someone with the information she is about to provide you. I knew enough to respond with "I'm not going to promise you that, just tell me what it is." She told me she slept with someone else. That hurt your boy.

Your Dad wasn't the Dad you feel is strong enough now. I was weak. SWV weak. Like XXL Freshman anything past 2012 weak. I was deeply hurt. Not just from the fact that she cheated on me. But because I was a virgin and I was saving myself for her. She went without me. That's like your mom coming home with the expectation that we were all going out to eat only to come home and find me throwing away the trash from Buffalo Wild Wings I WENT OUT to go get without her. Of course, it's not the exact same thing, but ask your mom how much that would hurt. I'm sure I'm not too far off.

But that wasn't it! I had to ask her, "So who was it? Do I know this person?" She said no. Then the bomb dropped. She said it was her youth pastor from her church. Bruh, I must've fell out! The funny side of me at the moment inside was like "Yo! They church got to take like 5 different offerings during service now!" But the angry side in me asked out loud, "Anything else you got to tell me?" I fucked up for asking that one kid. Lesson number three, stop while you're ahead. If you're already hurt on something, don't start digging for more, it only gets worse. And boy did it get worse. She then told me that she was pregnant by the guy. So not only did she cheat, she cheated with the pastor AND got pregnant. Son I know you think I'm bullshitting and making this up but on everything, I wouldn't lie to you about my past. I'm mad you laughing but hey, I can laugh about it now too so I understand. But when all that was dropped on me, I lost trust in a lot.

Women.

Church.

The future of being a father. All of that! Down the drain.

I continued my twenties with that same mind set of hurt and pain and didn't take much serious in other women that I decided to talk to at the time. I had to take time to myself to really love myself the way I needed to be loved and

35

to know what I really wanted and needed and I searched for that. But one day, I started having these dreams. These dreams kept coming over and over. It felt so real. In this particular dream I was walking around in my apartment with pictures of famous people's portraits all over the rooms. Samuel L Jackson, Morgan Freeman, Dave Chappelle, Tupac, Biggie Smalls! I know you're not knowledgeable of who these particular people are just yet, but trust me you will one day. They were all sorts of portraits in Black and white. I don't know why. But I kept seeing them over and over in my dreams.

Fast forward years later, I'm online on Facebook one day. Facebook is like a website you can talk with friends and people who think they are your friends and people who you've never met but guess what? You're friends! Go figure. That's our generation for you. But I saw these images, similar to those like in my dreams and I was captivated. I browsed and browsed for a long time before I found out who the artist was. The artist was your mom. Your mom was special enough to capture my eye without me even seeing who she was at first. Her images were like my dreams but in color. In a way you can say my life was dark before I met her, and it's true. She brought a different kind of light into my life this woman. We talked online back and forth for hours, days and days. The conversation was so real she was starting to doubt it I was even a real person. I had to video message her to show her I was real by saying something slick so she knew it was real. From then on, we just clicked. Love at first type. Getting to know your mom has been a joyous ride. Not the kind of ride like a rollercoaster you've been waiting to get on all day at the theme park. But a ride like with a hitchhiker from Craigslist on the way to California while you find out you both like Neo Soul music and enjoy good Hip Hop. It was bliss. It was different. So I had to approach different. I couldn't be the average guy I used to be anymore. I had to be more. I needed to be more. She was worth more and nothing less. So, the time came for us to meet and have our first date. At the time, I stayed in Austin after moving there a year earlier from Houston where your mom lived. It took two and a half hours to drive to her. I remember I left right after I was done at work getting off right at 5 o'clock. Kinda speeding down the road, I smoked a little weed on the way because I was nervous and I didn't want to fuck this up. I made sure to have the windows down a bit and spray the car down before I arrived because I knew she didn't smoke but I also didn't want that to be a turn off for her as well. This was my way of trying to make a good first impression.

What a guy right?

Well, I made it to her house and I must've waited outside for about 30 minutes before she finally came out. I thought it was a set up because here I am about 8 o'clock, outside in the dark, in the middle of the hood, waiting for a woman to come out a house I never been. This was very sketchy to say the least, but I was determined. When she came to the car I rushed to be the best gentleman I could be. I made sure to open the door for her, made sure she was fed and needless to say, she definitely did the same for me. She was beautiful! Her hair was longer than the line at the DMV. Her eyes were brown like aged pennies but worth so much more. And her smile could light up a room, or at least my life. As time passed, I got to know more of whom she was as a person and she got to know who I was as well. I shared my past and she shared hers. Found out we were both hoes and could admit that. But we found each other, a different kind of love. Our love.

As I found out who she was, I realized I REALLY had to be stronger and a much better man than I was because of the men in her past who didn't appreciate and respect her as much. It made me feel sad because all this time I was wasting other women's time, other guys were wasting hers. Read that last line again and see if you didn't just hear Aunt Karma say "Hmmmph". I said while I was wasting others' time, others were doing the same with your mom, possibly both prolonging the existence of both your mother and I's relationship in many ways. Time is a funny factor son. Your actions make up the test of it. You can affect your future as much as the next man. Let this just be a quick lesson into knowing to do right by women, not just for the benefit of getting something out of it, but because it's the right thing to do. If you're good to a woman and let's say it doesn't work out, it makes it easier for the next good man to be the one for her because now she at least knows what appreciation looks like. She knows what love looks like. She knows what respect and care look like. This is something I try to be the example of every day of my life while I'm around your mother, even without you around. Because the show doesn't start when you show up, the show goes on. Hell, the show started before you were born homeboy! But this is our show. It's live. It's real. Not staged. You may see some bloopers. Okay. You will see LOTS of bloopers. But that's because your Dad is a clown (not in the actual sense) and I love the moments that we have and can have in the future.

Somehow I feel like God blessed me with a son because the Most High knew that I could be trusted to duplicate myself. Part of me feels that guys who get daughters are meant to be tamed or calmed down from a certain life. So let's just say my past hasn't been that bad, hell at least you're here. And you're here with me. You're here with your mom. You're here with us. We are STILL learning to love each other each day in new ways. Sometimes it gets hard because of different reasons or emotions and we are trying to work through it all with honesty, open communication and understanding. And that's what I believe love is all about in relationships. We're working on us daily. We may not be the best example of what love can be, but I can guarantee you we're not the worst. We've seen worse, both of us with each of our parents and that helps us to be better to one another for the sake of what love can and should be. I've learned from my parents as an example of things TO do and what NOT to do. I'm going to be all the way real with you because you deserve honesty and truth. But you're strong enough to handle it. This I know.

But from my perspective, growing up in my parents' household I had to deal with a LOT of yelling. Not that it was always parties going on. Not at all. No one really came over. None of my friends. Not mostly because no one ever could, but because the yelling would be so at random that I didn't want my friends to know what our household was really like. We had everything we needed, my sister and I. Everything but peace. Something was wrong every week. And with the yelling, it was mostly your grandfather (my Dad) doing most of it. Well, I told you I would be honest. It was him doing the yelling. My mom was the quiet one of the two. That always seemed odd because they're both a Taurus sign. What's that? That's a type of zodiac symbol based on the time period you were born. To be a Taurus, you were symbolic of something like a ram, the head-butting type, headstrong and determined. But they were two different types. I guess mainly because they TOO had different upbringings than one another. Seeing my parents argue was not one of my favorite past times. Not by far! But it's what I had to deal with. This alone was something I said I would never want with my wife. If I couldn't communicate to the point of understanding, I had to reevaluate HOW I was communicating in a way she would understand. That's a sign of empathy which is a very strong trait to have as a Cancer sign. Me and you are both Cancers son and that alone is why I feel we would always have an understanding of not only one another but others as well. Right now, you're at the stage of pulling on other baby's hair and biting. I'm quite sure that understanding of empathy hasn't kicked in just yet, but it will. This I know. With your mom and I, we have our differences and similarities, like anyone else. I have my faults and she has hers. I have my great qualities and so does she. With love, I'll say you have to make sure the good outweighs the bad. If it doesn't, get out! Don't think twice.

My dad was divorced once before meeting my mom. And your mother's parents were both divorced before meeting each other (your grandparents on your mother's side aren't legally married anymore but they're still together). I know, weird. But that's their love. I'm not sure whose love is stronger between your mother and I, it might even be neck and neck but on different terms. I get my artistic side shown more through her. She gets her business side shown more through me. That's one of the ways we inspire one another. Honestly, you have to know even good things don't always last. If for some reason your mother and I split, it's not your fault. It's not hers. It's not mine. It's just the differences became too much to where the bad outweighed the good. Your mother and I both come from different road maps to show us what love can and shouldn't be. Neither of those maps were perfect in our eyes but it's what we've been given. In all things of life, knowledge and all, you have to take those things that seem good to you and apply it to your life to fit what's best for you to do. I love your mom and she loves me. That's all we know. Again, we're learning and we're not perfect. But this is our love. Welcome home.

It's Okay to Quit

There's an old saying that goes "Winners never quit and quitters never win". I'm here to tell you that may not be exactly true. Now I'm sure you think your Dad is amazing at a lot of things. You see me working on music at home. You see me painting art with your mother. You see me out here grinding with my other business ventures. Hell you probably think we're rich. Don't play yourself child. We're not rich, but we're not broke either. Just know you will always be taken care of one way or another. And you'll have a lot of things, lots of toys, clothes, and stuffed animals (I loved stuffed animals as a child). Yet these things will come and go so it's best not to get attached to material objects or even people rather. They ALL come and go. But while you have anything or anyone in your life, what you MUST do is learn to appreciate whatever it is. Appreciation can take you a long way.

What is appreciation? I can give you an example better than I can define it. So take this for instance, let's say you wanted ice cream. I ask you what kind would you like, you just say you don't care, you just want ice cream. I say cool. Now we're in the car with me, your mother, your brother and cousins and we all stop for ice cream. Everybody gets a vanilla ice cream cone including you. For some odd reason you want to cry about the one thing you said you wanted because it wasn't what you expected or the flavor wasn't the right one. I say give the ice cream to your brother. Your brother likes ice cream and he's going to be sure to make sure you watch every minute of him enjoy it. Seconds after the horror that is watching someone else enjoy what you had, you now decide that you want it back. That my guy is what we call not having appreciation. You didn't want for something you had, you didn't enjoy something you lost, you had every opportunity to care and be content with what you wanted, but the moment you can't anymore, you cry about it. That's not cool. That's never cool. Take that small lesson and apply it to a relationship because most likely if you're a better human than me, you're going to be with someone one day. You might love that person and then you might stop. That person might leave you because you stopped. That's not a moment to cry. That's a moment to learn that you did not appreciate what you had until it's gone. It happens to the best of us kiddo. Try not to have to learn that lesson first hand and appreciate all that you have, because no matter what you have, there is always someone else who WISHES they had that and WILL appreciate that very thing whether it is love, a toy or even something like an opportunity.

It's okay to stop doing what doesn't interest you anymore though so never feel like you're obligated to stick with anything because you started a commitment to it. Just know all actions come with reactions and you may not like the reactions but just appreciate them as they come. Why tell you this? I tell you this because I've stopped many things I started. I was a professional quitter. If quitting was a sport, your dad was an all-state MVP champion of them all. I didn't appreciate a lot of things I had in life at times. Some of those things were relationships with others, some of them were opportunities, and some were just objects I didn't see value in anymore. I paid the price for each of them. Most I remember about quitting anything was mainly sports. I like sports more on TV than actually being a part of it, but that's me. Though I feel we're very similar you and I, you might surprise me and say "Dad, I want to do hockey," or "Dad, I want to be in the Olympics". That would impress me that your goal would be the Olympics! I think that's as big of a dream as someone being an astronaut. I never met either one but it would nice to know I raised one. But your Dad on the other hand, the first thing I ever tried was karate. I took the first class and was bored because we weren't doing much in there but learning and watching. That was already boring to me. At that time, I was about that action but wasn't seeing any of it like in the movies. I wasn't patient enough with karate. Most importantly, I didn't appreciate the opportunity to have the knowledge of learning more. Why did I quit? Simply because karate practice was on Thursday nights and so was WWE Smackdown (that's a wrestling show that came on TV). I didn't want to miss wrestling for the world! I loved watching wrestlers like The Rock and Stone Cold Steve Austin talk smack. Or watch Mankind and Rey Mysterio Jr. taking it to the limits with putting their lives on the line or even watching Goldberg just kick ass! I loved wrestling and I thought being in karate would be a step towards that, but once I tried it, it wasn't the same. I just enjoyed watching fighting and more so Kung Fu movies, especially anything with Jackie Chan. Sidebar: Go watch the movie Rumble in The Bronx and tell me that movie isn't bad ass. I dare you.

But then I got older and guess what? Yep. I quit watching wrestling too. My favorites mainly retired or died off so I didn't see an interest anymore. I don't regret quitting karate, obviously I wasn't as interested in it and plus that saved my Dad like $30 a week from not having to pay for something I wouldn't appreciate. I'm sure he appreciated that. Your grandfather's not cheap like me but he does like to afford things and not spending $30 on karate meant spending $30 for something else more important like food on the table and other things. If you can do me any favors like that, I'd appreciate it. It's okay to quit. Don't force what you don't feel is meant for you to do. So what other sports did I try? Shiiiiiit... what didn't I try? I tried football, at the time I was allergic to grass and I was itching like crazy so that was a no go. I tried out for basketball, but didn't make the team. Can you believe I didn't have hops? Talk about Black Men Can't Jump. All my other peers were great at it, just not me. But one thing I can say is that I was ALWAYS good at stealing the ball. Just no hops. I wasn't really good at shooting but I never gave myself the full opportunity to try. Why? It was because I quit that too. Oh! But let me tell you how I quit at track! Now running was something your dad was good at. In fact, I loved to run since elementary. I remember in like 4th grade there were these Mexican triplets, the Cantus everyone knew them as. Only two of them looked the same and the third looked more like a cousin. Weird shit I know. But I remember we were all at Physical Education class (known as P.E.) and we were doing a race as a class. We all took off. It seemed like I was doing well for a little bit. Next thing you know, one of the triplets passed me up and I mean quickly. I think he may even had lapped me. Then the second triplet went by. I thought to myself "Of course, they look alike". Then the third triplet passed me up and I was like "No way! You're not even related!" All three of them beat me and I came in 4th place in the race. That was a memorable time for me because I got beat by a family and to me that was like a symbolization of them sticking together. I never told them that's what I got from their bond, but it is what it is. I didn't quit that race, but I didn't win. And that's okay son. It's good for you to know that kind of lesson as well. Sometimes in life, you won't win and that's okay. It's how you comeback that matters.

Fast forward years later to like 10th grade, and this is how my comeback failed. It was track team tryouts. I wanted to be like the other few Black kids I saw at school. They were fast and I knew I was fast too. I used to run faster than kids on 18 speed bicycles. I used to chase my mom's car when she drove away from home (those were the times I really didn't want her to go). I was just extremely fast. So I wanted to hang with the big boys. Tryouts came and I was ready for whatever. They gave everyone a choice between hurdles or pole vaults. I didn't feel like running with anything in my hands because I felt it would slow me down. Plus I was always told not to run with scissors, how safe could a pole be right? Just go to YouTube sometime and type in Pole Vault bloopers and see what happens. Exactly! So I chose hurdles. I mean how hard could it be? We ran and jumped on everything back in the neighborhood. It couldn't be that hard to jump over something. So I thought. Here I am, in line with the others. Its tryout time and my time to show them what I got. That whistle blew and I took off! And shiiiiiiit…when I tell you almost everyone else was way much faster, I'm not lying. They took off like a jet at an air show. This wasn't one of those "slow and steady wins the race" kind of moments. I was getting washed. But I kept going. Then…the hurdles came. I jumped over the first one.

Cleared it!

I must've thought this was going to be a breeze! But the second hurdle wasn't too far away from the first one and your Dad was not prepared. It was higher than I expected and let's just say I busted my ass more than I wanted to that day. I mean I got hung! Hurdle all on top of me and everything. I'm lying on the ground getting bullied by plastic and metal trying to get up off my back. Shit was wild! I wasn't embarrassed but I knew right then, nope! I'm done. I quit. Never again. I just walked off. Didn't talk to the coaches ever again, just walked off and kept going. Only thing I DIDN'T quit was walking away.

I didn't even look back. I wasn't embarrassed, maybe. I look back at that moment and laugh, I have to.

Your dad is the type that grew up watching Maximum Exposure, a show where people took major hits crashing and burning by doing things like driving, skateboarding, riding bikes and such and busting their ass. It was comedy to me! So when things like that happened to me, I just can't help but to laugh at my pain. I knew that track wasn't for me so I quit and guess what, that's okay. I knew I would somehow find my passion one day. It just wasn't that day. So you're going to quit some things son. It's a part of life's journey into finding your purpose. You got to try different things. Some things you're going to stick to and some you just aren't. Sometimes you might even come to a point where you don't WANT to quit something but feel like you have to. Those are the harder choices and most likely with the right mind, those choices are the ones that help mold you to be a better person. You might be hanging with the wrong people in life and notice that you're meant to go in a different direction than they are. You might feel like you love those people or they love you and feel obligated to be around. Life isn't a bank and you're not in debt to anyone but yourself. You owe yourself the chance to be better than you were the day before. Part of that being better may have to be letting go of others around you, quitting your dedication of so much time to what could be negative or not productive to your wellbeing. But guess what? It's okay to quit. You remember I told you that you would have lots of things in life? Yeah, changes are amongst the few at the top of the list of things you will have the most out of. So get ready for that! Your favorite shoes, you might outgrow those. Your favorite shirt, you might not fit anymore. Your favorite song, you might not like that artist anymore. Your favorite color might not have the same meaning anymore. Things change, people change, and feelings change too. One thing that might change is your choice in what you want to be when you grow up. I know for sure my choice changed a bunch of times. Here's a list of things your dad wanted to be growing up:

-a cop

-a terrorist

-an assassin

-a lawyer

-a teacher

-a clown

-a rapper

-the President of the United States

-Raven Symone's or Solange's baby daddy

And here we are today, I am none of those things. Although I'm still working on Solange, I haven't quit that just yet. But for the most part, my choices have changed over time. I quit wanting to be those things. And guess what? It's okay to quit. What's meant to be will be and you will find yourself. I know it seems like I'm heavily endorsing the idea of quitting like it's the cool thing to do. It's not the best thing I would want you to be, for God's sake PLEASE find some kind of foundation for yourself. But I just want you to know that it's okay to quit because something greater is always meant for you, but only if you want it. I mean you REALLY have to want it bad enough to not quit. What people tend to forget about the idea of quitting is the idea of returning. Quitting doesn't make it the end of anything. It's only a decision of a choice in pause. The rejection of returning during a delay creates the quit within the action itself (damn that's good stuff, write that down). I might start a plate of food, get tired and quit eating. That doesn't make me a failure, it that just makes me full. Now when I'm hungry again, I have two options. I can either, go back to that same plate and finish it or I can go get something else. You always have a choice as long as you live to go back to something you quit or didn't finish. Life gives you opportunities daily; it's what you CHOOSE to do with the time given that tells the story of how and what your life will be. Whether it is love, goals, food, (and boy do I love food so I understand) go for what you know. Trust your gut. Follow your mind and listen to your heart. Let those two functions in your body get you the point where you know who you are and what you really want to do in life. I can't make that decision for you. Your mother can't make that decision for you. Only you can. But whatever it is you feel you are destined to do, you'll know. How you ask? You'll know when you quit quitting. You're welcome.

Kanye Was Right

In life, you might be taught that there are two sides to every story, the ying and the yang, the good and the bad and that's it. I want you to know son that that is not entirely true. There is always an in between. Learn to question that trial and error of the either true and untrue with the existence of the in between. Learn to push the envelope or the idea of concept you yet to understand because you feel there is more to know. Your questioning can also develop more understanding for those giving you information to interpret what they are telling you doesn't even make sense to them anymore. That right there is taking control of your thoughts.

It's best to think for yourself, and yes you may get information from your mother and I or anyone else rather, but that doesn't always make us right. That information given to you whether it be small like "Don't forget to wear a jacket, it's going to be cold, or something big like "Hey! Keep your credit utilization on your accounts at 10% and paid off monthly and you'll have a great credit score", that information is for you to intake and use if you see fit. But just know whatever you choose to do with us, your parents' guidance; it is ALWAYS in your best interest. I just want you to know that. You can be whatever you want. You can be a low life scum bag if you want or you can be the world's smartest man, or anything in between. Just find your purpose and be creative with it. Creativity takes you so far in life, trust me. I can't stress to you enough how important creativity is. It's something unique I already see in you. You're so fast! You're so smart. You're so in tune with the things around you. I can even tell with the things you do and how you began to teach yourself to stand and climb, you're hella creative and I love it!

There are many people who taught me directly and indirectly on being creative. My all-time favorite of teachers of creativity is named Kanye West. Many people adore him. Many people hate him. He's a music artist, producer, designer and much more. He's a very creative person that just happens to be right. About what, you're probably wondering. Who is Kanye? Why is he so important? What's so special about this guy? Well let me just take you back to my teenage years (you'll hopefully love this period of your life growing up). He's who I think is a prime example of past, present and future so just hear me out okay. One day I was riding with my mom around town as she was shopping various places. She made a stop at the Family Thrift Store on N. Shepherd one day and I didn't want to go inside. Crazy thing is: for one, I couldn't steal anything in there because they had nothing I liked. And two, I didn't want to get clothes from a thrift store back then because I spoiled myself and felt I only wanted new clothes on my back. I was an ass. I shop almost ONLY at thrift stores now. I'm probably going to be just like my mom getting older now and hopefully you won't think you're too good for thrift store clothes like I did (Life hack: People try on clothes at the mall and big stores and return them all the time so you will most likely always wear someone else's clothes, just get it cheaper and save as much you can ALWAYS). But that store stop that day changed my life.

As we stopped at the store, I asked my mom if I can stay in the car. She said yes. For some reason, the public rule is to never leave your kids in the car but they never determine at what age you should start. I guess it wasn't one of my mother's concerns that day, and neither was it mine. I kept some of the windows down and I turned the radio on. It was 97.9 The Box and I hear the DJ introduce a new artist by the name of Kanye West making waves. They explain that this guy was in a car accident, almost lost his life, had his jaw wired shut and that he was a well-known producer for other artists. I never heard of this guy but it had to be something special about him for the radio to share his story before playing his music. So then they played his song. The song was called "Through The Wire". Now I'm thinking before they play this song that this guy was from Houston and they were breaking his record out on the radio so I was heavily in tune. Then the song starts. "Dun, dun, dun, duuuuuuuuuuuuuuuuun. Through the wireeeee." All you could hear was this chipmunk sounding sample of which was later to find out to be Chaka Khan. This beat was something new and different than what was normally played on the radio. And then Kanye started rapping. Oh man! The bars he was spitting and the flow, it was just so new and like magic to my ears (Your generation might appreciate an artist like Kanye, but if not, I understand).

"I drink a boost for breakfast, an Ensure for dizzert.

Somebody order pancakes, I just sip the sizzurp.

That right there can drive a sane man bizerk.

Not to worry, Mr. H to the Izzo's back to wizzerk."

Like that was the first line I ever heard from this guy and it was just so damn cool to me. Let me break that down for you the best I know how to relate it. So this guy has his jaw wired shut, still determines to rap about his life in details and it comes down to this? If you didn't know son, Boost and Ensure are these kinds of drinks that you drink as meals. When you're in the hospital and in a certain position where you can't eat, you get fed meals through a tube. This was his way of eating in description. "Sizzurp" is a common term for cough syrup sometimes known as Promethazine or "lean", famous known drink of choice for a lot of rappers in Southern culture (I definitely don't recommend this). Going "bizerk" is a term to describe crazy, which ironically in his life, people think he has. And "H to the Izzo" was a very popular song that hit the charts by the artist known as Jay-Z, which is now coined to be Hip Hop's first billionaire. Kanye West produced that song and many, many more for Jay-Z, helping him get to the top of the game as some consider. That last line was letting us know that yes he produced that song and he's back in the music game working, also letting us know not to worry, he's doing better now. The song "Through the Wire" continues to describe the pain and the effects he and others felt around him during his accident but finishes the song with "But I'm a champion, so I turned tragedy to triumph, made music that's fire, spit my soul through the wire". I was done at that point! I was like "Yooooo! Whoever this Houston artist is HAS to make it. Then the song went off and the radio DJ was like "Alright that was

Kanye West with Through the Wire, new artist out of Chicago…".

Damn!!!

I thought Houston had a legend right there! I was crushed that this guy wasn't from Houston but I was so proud to hear a song like that on the radio with such a rich story in rhymes. I haven't felt like that since Biggie Smalls with the song "Juicy" (you'll have to look up that one at a later time, right now this is about Kanye). This was a hint of creativity that sparked me along because I knew I wanted to do music and this guy solidified it for me that this was something I really wanted to do. His sounds influenced me to create something new and different in a way that I would know I'm unique, not everyone else.

With creativity, you don't always want to base it on the idea of other's viewpoint. Just tell your story. Fuck what everyone else things. Just do you. You see, when you're creating things, you have the responsibility of helping society to become better or helping society to be worse. You have the chance to fix a problem or create a worse one. Problems exist and you will never be able to avoid them. Money might make it seem that your problems will go away where in fact; money will only make your problems possibly better but no less. Love might also make it seem that it will decrease your problems but it will only divert your attention to other problems you will now be responsible of like care, constant attention, respect, or other traits pertaining to your relationship that you had no clue you lacked. But having the ability to create and be innovative in something old gives you the chance to be responsible in doing things your way; a new way. When something is new to everyone, you'll understand that their opinions of what and how you do something that's never been done can mean absolutely less. Fuck it! That's when you just really go for it and nothing can stop you but you. Kanye said it best, "I could let these dream killers kill my self-esteem, or use my arrogance as a steam to power my dreams". Don't be influenced by the naysayers who say you can't do this and that. It's negative and you don't want that in your life. Some people tell Kanye West "Man, you have the power to influence a lot of people." But let Kanye tell it, he'll say "I have the power to not be influenced." That's the ideal of what I like about Kanye. He started breaking out into the music industry as a music producer, mainly playing the background.

He continuously told his peers and others alike "Yo! You gotta hear my rhymes! I can rap too!" but many just looked at him as a producer and told him to stick to that. If he continued to listen to those same people, he would have never made other groundbreaking songs that were on his debut album such as "Jesus Walks" and "All Falls Down", which both were on the radio like crazy! Yes there was a Hip Hop song on the radio about Jesus, sometimes even played after or before Lil Jon and the Eastside Boys "I Don't Give a Fuck". The radio was and still is a crazy kind of thing as far as what's normally played. (Sidebar: Try to find genuine music that makes you feel good but has good meaning and more of a positive message. You'll find ratchet music which is okay, but find your balance in the alternative as well). When people told him he couldn't have a song about Jesus on a Hip Hop station that made him go even harder into doing so.

Religion makes a lot of people feel iffy about what to say or not say out loud or in public. Kanye doesn't give a fuck. He knows he's responsible for what he says, but he doesn't care about him saying it because he knows it needs to be said. Going against the grain of the norm is what being creative is about. What can you do differently that will set a new standard in the field you're creating? What will have your creation stand out and get noticed versus getting added to the pile of what already exists? Will it have substance? Will it have meaning? What will the substance and meaning be to you? That's what matters. Not what others think, but what you think about you and your actions. Does it serve purpose? Is it good for you? Will it plant a good seed for the world? Ask yourself and always answer yourself honestly.

As I mentioned before, Kanye had a song called "All Falls Down" and this one hit home for your Dad. I was entering college as a Freshman around the time this album came out that was ironically titled "College Dropout". The last thing I wanted to do was go to college and quit this too. Tell me why this song came at the right time too! First few lines states,

"Man I promise, she's so self conscious.
She has no idea what she's doing in college.
That major that she majored in don't make no money.
But she won't drop out, her parents will look at her funny.
Now, tell me that ain't insecure.
The concept of school seems so secure.
Sophomore three years ain't picked a career.
She like fuck it, I'll just stay down here and do hair."
That was TOO real for me! And if that wasn't already enough, he ended the song with this,
"It seems, we living the American dream
But the people highest up got the lowest self esteem
The prettiest people do the ugliest things

For the road to riches and diamond rings.

We shine because they hate us

Floss cause they degrade us.

We trying to buy back our 40 acres.

And for that paper, look how low we a'stoop

Even if you in a Benz, you still a nigga in a coupe."

(Sidebar: I thought the very last line was "Even if you ain't in a band, you still a nigga in a group, which I thought was still thought provoking, but eh well).

But to be honest, I DIDN'T know what I was doing in college other than just picking a major that had something to do with what I was already doing. Before college in high school I would always draw houses, big houses! I'd draw houses with big windows and a nice gate. Maybe I'd draw houses with a balcony outside the bedroom window. Sometimes I'd draw houses with lots of cars outside. What I was doing was drawing what I wanted my life to be like when I got older. My idea at the time wasn't I want to be an Architect. I was just drawing my vision of what I wanted for me and my family. I was scared to tell my parents that I didn't know what I wanted to go to school for so since I was already drawing houses that I was good at, I just said I'll go and study Architecture. I fucked up. When I got into college it wasn't all what I expected, at least not the classes for that major. I worked 2 or three jobs at times while taking 18 hours a week of classes I didn't care about. I worked so much because I didn't want to ask my parents for anything else. I was in heavy resentment for a long time. I went years with stress migraines which sometimes kept me from going to class at all. I skipped my Architecture classes sometimes and instead I would just go to the library and be creative with my time. I started doing more of what I ACTUALLY wanted to do and that was music. I started downloading music videos and created my own music video countdown shows. That made me feel good about myself because I was doing what I liked. I would also stay in my room most of the days and work on producing music. I would sample lots of older music like Kanye West, but I would do it my own way. And studying history led me to look deeper into History that connected WITH me more personally.

I would then go back and visit my parents' house during college, we would sometimes as a family even when Aunts and Uncles came over and play this game called Phase 10. I looked up who was the creator of this game since we enjoyed playing it so much, and what did you know? It was a Black man who created it. I probably would have never known that if it weren't for the History classes I was taking in college teaching me to go back and research what interests you. Since I saw that, I thought, "If a Black man can create a game years ago, I wonder what kind of game I can create that would be played years from now. Back in February 2011, I created a game called Stereotypes! We played it in the college dorm room to test it out and it was phenomenally hilarious! It took years to make changes to the card topics and logo and design, but I finally released in on the market online in 2017, six years after creating something I made while skipping class. This game got me recognition and in places I never imagined. It's still selling today and is one of the reasons you have been fed and I had History class to thank for all of the inspiration. I wanted to change my major to History so I could be a History teacher and change other young people's idea on the past the way it was taught to my generation (the incorrect way). My parents didn't take that idea well and said I should just stick it out.

That sucked big balls!

I figured I'd have the kind of parents that would understand if I said I didn't want to do something with my life and wanted to do something else that I saw would serve a greater purpose, and they would be behind me. But they weren't and from that day I knew I would never be that type of parent to my child, to you. I will ALWAYS listen to what you say and take consideration of what you seriously want out of life and will help you the best way I know how every step of the way. It took a while for me to realize I had to stop living life for others and start living for myself and determine my own happiness. Or as Kanye would say "I refuse to accept other people's ideas of happiness for me, as if there's a "one size fits all" standard for happiness". I've taken a few shots to the face to know for the future what's right to do with my kids forward.

So, if you want to be a clown, you can bet your ass I'm going to help you with a cold business plan to take over the business of being funny. You want to be a chef, I'll never throw you out the kitchen and we'll go eat wherever you like (we'll call it research… write offs). Whatever it is you want to do in life, just know you have me and your mother's back and we need you to know that. We can't do everything for you, but we will always do our best in showing you the way to find out how to get it done, no matter what.

So as time passes by year after year, album after album, Kanye just gets bigger and bigger as a star. What some people never saw in him, he saw in himself the whole time. "I'm the greatest!" he would say. People would ask, "Who do you think you are?" and he'd reply "I just TOLD you who I am. I am a God. Perhaps you would have felt better if I said I am a nigga?" Kanye just pushed the envelope saying a lot of what those who would understand it to be groundbreaking or brave whereas to others not in agreeance would say he is arrogant, cocky, or ignorant.

If your mind is free to understand where people are coming from not on a path of to agree or disagree but just to understand, then you can better understand the comprehension of a lot of things. Those with this kind of understanding will be best to keep around you in your creative state. Again, you're a Cancer. So you're naturally creative, one of the most creative signs of them all. It will be easy to get thrown off your path of creativity by those who lack understanding and are around just to deny you or bring you down. You will also have the tendency to be sensitive of other's feelings. That's also a downfall of your strength of empathy. You understand where others do not. Don't let that be a reason why you STOP doing what you feel you are destined to do. You are powerful! And you too have the power not to be influenced. Your power lies within the greatness of which you set it upon. You're responsible in finding that. Know yourself. Do what you feel and remember, follow your mind, but listen to your heart. Make every moment count, chances are what you're about to create may be the beginning of something greater. So in the words of Kanye, "If you have the opportunity to play this game of life you need to appreciate every moment. A lot of people don't appreciate the moment until it's passed".

And the Beat Goes On

You know that feeling you get when you hear a song and you're bobbing your head up and down because you really feel the beat of the tune? I see you do it all the time and it gives me joy!

Why?

Because I do that all the time!

That's when I really know the music is good. There's this point where the music starts to jam so good that I'm bobbing my head to the point I might break my neck and my lip is stuck like you just let out one of those farts even YOU can't stand the smell of. Yeah, that's a fire ass song right there.

I've been graced with the opportunity to hear so much music in my lifetime thus far and I've been able to learn from every single song. There are at least 5 songs in my lifetime that I just want to share with you that helped mold me majorly in life along the way. These songs may do the same for you but at least you will be able to see how they make me the person that I am today. Now before I give you this list, don't just set my life to JUST these songs, there are plenty of them I adore, but these are just some of the ones that I remember most that mean more to me at this current moment than before. So the list goes (in no particular order):

1.   Alexander O'Neal- Love Makes No Sense
2.   Little Brother- All for You
3.   Common- It's Your World
4.   Chrissy Depauw- Chance
5.   Musiq Soulchild- GiveMoreLove

I'll explain these songs and their importance, but first let me take you on a journey of how I got into music myself. Your dad is a music producer. Yes, like Kanye West (just not as big…headed). I haven't traveled all over the world with my music with big name artists that I've worked for. I am still on the beginner's level of advancement. I may very well always be on the beginner's level, not because I'll never get to where I'm famous everywhere I go, but because there's always so much to learn. And although I've only been producing about 11 years, most people in the music industry have been at it for about 10+ years before they are recognized majorly for what they are talented in. I just focus on having fun and enjoying the sounds I can mix and create for me to listen to. I used to work very close with music artists at their beginning stage and it has worked well for me. I've learned a lot from each individual as far as creativity, content, grinding, ideas, and more. Every individual is unique like you and I so it's always good to be versatile and soak up knowledge from one another and implement that into your daily life where you see fit.

I started off in high school with this guy named Dietrich. We were the go-to beat bangers. Beat bangers were the guys who always had writing utensils on them, not for signatures silly, but to drop a beat at ANY point in time. We could be waiting for the bus outside by the window, a beat is going down! We could be in DMC (this is detention known as Dead Man's Corner, a place for kids being punished) and the teacher steps out, a beat is going down! We could be at all the lunches in the cafeteria (because no one took 4th period serious), a beat is going down! No matter what, we surrounded ourselves with music and people who enjoyed it. Kids would freestyle rap about their day, different teachers, their dreams, clothes and all. It was like hearing a daily report by voice to a beat, our beat. I could be working a beat so good to the point where the pen breaks but it wasn't a problem because Dietrich might pull out another one from behind his ear right on time for me to hop back on without missing a beat. These times were amazing and this was a joyous time in our teenage years. I'm really hoping you have some kind of dope experience like this that you can remember in your earlier years when you get older.

I sometimes took my Dad's recorder from home (he never knew because I was always sure to put it right back in place) so that I could record some of these sound sessions at school. I'd take the mic attached to the cord and put it on the table so the mic could pick up the bass from us beating on the tables. I'd go back home and listen to them and make a mix CD for only me to listen to. I really wish I had some of those recordings to this day, but I know what was left is now gone from damaged hard drives (thanks Harvey). This was just my beginning stage of making any kind of music. It wasn't until I got to college where I met your Uncle (my best friend) Kris. He's the reason I was able to practice making beats officially. I knew he was going to be my best friend because when I was moving into our dorm room on campus, he had two things in his room as I walked by that I saw was a strong indicator. He had an MPC drum pad beat machine to make music and the season DVDs for Family Guy on his dresser. Family Guy was all I pretty much watched at the time for comedy so we were going to get along very well I knew. Kris gave me the music program for free to get started making music and from then on in between every class of mine (sometimes during class) I would work on music in my room. It took a lot of practice to get familiar with the program enough to be comfortable with it, but I did. I didn't quit at that because I really enjoyed it. I found something I was good at and didn't stop working on my craft. That's something I would love for you to remember son, whatever your craft that you will be good at, continuously work on it to get better and hopefully it too can gain you income or at least be the stepping stone into moving you forward to better things. Now with producing, I got my vibe, sound or personality mainly from those five songs I listed earlier. So let's go back and I'll explain the details of each.

With Alexander O'Neal and the song "Love Makes No Sense", from the album titled *"Love Makes No Sense"*, I remember this particular album well because it's one of the few albums I would always take from my dad's CD holder at home. He really didn't like for us to touch his things, whether he was home or not. So being the rebel you're learning I am, I touched it like a motherfucker! And I was jamming! Sometimes I knew the schedule of my parents and their working so well that I knew it was a period of time I had before they were coming back home. So in that period of time sometimes I'd take that album and play it on the loud stereo running and dancing back and forth throughout the house. I mean I was dancing like I was on Soul Train, hitting those 80's and 90s vibe type dances. These words from this song hit me though, even as a young child.

"When love is good, it's really good.
But when love is bad, it feels so bad.
I know, no matter
Come what may, I never stray
In all the joy, and all the pain."

Those were fucking bars! It might sound basic but that makes so much sense. People when they love, they can love with all their heart. Other people can see their love in good times and think, "Wow, that's the kind of love I want!" People can see that same love go sour and in bad times think, "Wow, that's not the kind of love I need in my life." Funny they can recognize that it's still love but it's not love in the form of where it needs to be for both parties involved. Sometimes things aren't the best when it comes to love. I've found that out in many relationships, including me and your mother's. Let's be honest, there are times where I love her to the moon and back and there's nothing I wouldn't do for her because nothing gives me the kind of joy to see her happy, even us happy together. But sometimes she isn't the best with her words or emotions and the mix of that being expressed without knowing how to express them can be dangerous territory. If I didn't know that about your mom, I might have been a worse type of guy and you'd be reading about how

Eminem's "Just the Two of Us" is my all-time favorite song (although negative, that song does jam). But I understand her and songs can teach you a lot about not only yourself but others as well in the past, present and future. That's what it does for me, especially this song.

With Little Brother "All For You", coming from the album titled *"The Minstrel Show"*, this song is just an incredible expression of a feeling between father and son to me. The first verse describes a feeling of being raised without a father and being left neglected for so long. The hurt and confusion is something I was hearing yet glad I wasn't going through. I could have empathy and understand because so many of my close friends did not have fathers around.

Sometimes it's a deeper story to why fathers aren't around. Sometimes the kids don't know the hardships between parents and resentment builds up over years with no concept to grasp of how or why. Though being without a father can hurt, it's always my goal in life to never let you feel that pain. I would rather me be dead and gone before that happens, yet if ever in the case I were to die before you grow up to really know me, hopefully this book can rest your nerve in knowing I tried every step of the way. The second verse of "All For You" hit even more home for me because this was the ultimate feeling I had in a past relationship and sometimes I get the feeling with your mother when we're not on our best of days. The verse goes,

"I was looking at your photograph, amazed how I favored you.
I remember being young and wanting to play with you
Cause you was a wild and crazy dude,
And I would understand why my mama couldn't ever stay with you.
From the roots to the branch to the leaves
They say apples don't fall far from the trees.
Used to find it hard to believe, and I swore that I would.
Always hold my family as long as I could, but damn.
Our memories can be so misleading.
It's misery, I hate to see history repeating.
Thought you were the bad guy, but I guess that's why
Me and my girl split and my son is leaving.
I did chores, did bills and did dirt,
But I, swear to God I tried to make that shit work.
Till I, came off tour to an empty house,
With all the dressers and the cabinets emptied out.
I think I must've went insane,
Thinking I was in love but really in chains.
Trapped to this girl,
Through the two year old who carried my name.
I tried to stop tripping.
But yo' I couldn't and the plot thickened.
That shit affected me, largely.
Cause I know a lot of people want me
To fail as a father and the thought of that haunts me.
Especially when I check my rear view mirror
And don't see him in his car seat.
So the next time it's late at night
And I'm laid up with the woman I'm gone make my wife
Talking about how we gone make a life,
I'm thinking about child support, alimony, visitation rights.
Cause that's the only outcome if you can't make it right.
Pissed off with your children, feeling the same pain.
So Pop, how could I blame you cause you couldn't maintain?
I did the same thing… the same thing."

76

Damn... I know right? It's like when you read lyrics as it were poetry, it seems deeper in meaning because you can take your time to speak and hear those words slowly. This verse explains how a man as a child thought of his father being out and about yet growing older to be that same type of person and seeing the effects of fatherhood now on both sides of the spectrum. Yet, this time he feels an understanding of the full circle of mistakes he made in his life through the cycle that was not broken.

Luckily in my mid-aged 20's, I paid heavy attention to that since the first time hearing this song. I was with an ex of mine a couple relationships before your mom and needless to say things weren't always the best of the best on both sides. I was wilder then and I had trust issues I was still dealing with and she was a single mother but not the best of types I would expect out of a woman, at least not for me. I tried to make the relationship work in many ways doing best of what I knew how. I would sit and talk with my dad and he would explain to me his past in dating before getting married the first time. Not saying he was "out there" or anything, but he did say he talked to many women, many types and ethnicities. I did the same thing except I decided not to share with him my experiences. I wasn't too proud of my "achievements" especially hearing how it got him nowhere and I felt the same about my path.

With my dad also explaining how his first marriage went sour with abuse and all, I could see that same form in the relationship I was in at the time. We would argue till our voices were out like we'd been at a Beyonce' concert singing every word. We'd fight until I'd realize that her daughter was watching and I'd leave because I didn't want to further damage the setting than what was set at the time. I wasn't the best man for her and she wasn't the best woman for me. That was that. And that song showed me what my life would be like had I continued like my dad with his first marriage. Instead, my dad found refuge or a "second chance" rather in his second marriage with my mother.

Growing up, I told myself I want my first marriage to be like my dad's second, but without the yelling and problems. You can do without the yelling all day but sad to say, you will NEVER have a relationship without problems. You may have one with better problems than before, which is what I would say your mother and I have right now. The most we argue about is communicating how we feel in a timely matter and being mad because we did or said something that made one feel uncomfortable, or my favorite kind of mad, missing each other or just plain hungry. We don't fight (thank God), we're not abusive, we're faithful, honest and caring individuals with each other and that's what I'm grateful for. I can hear songs about love and think, "Oh that's us!" I'm very grateful for artists like Little Brother who can be transparent about their feelings in ways most rappers don't in which the everyday listener who may be going through similar things can take others mistakes as their own and learn from them or adjust to avoid them as much as possible. That's the kind of music you'd find in my collection (if you ever so decide to try to sneak through and listen).

With Common and the song titled "It's Your World" from the Be album, this was the ending of an ending and ironically the beginning of a beginning. I'll explain. So, remember I told you about that girlfriend earlier in this book who slept with her pastor and had the baby? Yeah, when I say I was hurt, hurt, I'm so for real. I wouldn't wish that kind of random pain for anyone's heart. Not even yours my boy. Now someone may not be faithful to you in life, hell, you might not be faithful to them, but don't take these types of things to heart like I did. I felt vengeful, sorry and really felt like giving up a lot, especially at life. That's right. I had my first taste of depression and I didn't even know it until later. After that situation with old girl, I didn't even want to be in the same state as her anymore.

I was 17 and decided to fly away to San Francisco for my birthday week. I went to stay with my cousin Murphy and it was nonetheless a learning experience. Murphy was the closest male cousin on both sides of my family, and we weren't even that close. But he was the closest to somebody that I felt would understand me. I told him what happened and he understood well because he was a social worker for the youth there in the Bay Area. He dealt with far worse kids than me but he knew how to handle my thought processing. So knowing I liked music, he took me to the largest record store in the city.

There I bought only one album, the Common *"Be"* album. This album to me is landmarked as one of the greatest albums ever because it's the ONLY one fully produced by two of three of my favorite music producers, J Dilla and Kanye West (third place is 9th Wonder). This album to me saved my life because even though my cousin was talking life to me, I needed to hear something, feel something enough for me to stay on this earth a little longer. I needed purpose. Murphy and I got a bite to eat on Mission St. and we went to go get chiropractic massages from his therapist. It was free for me because it was my first time in California, plus Murphy did Jiu-Jitsu as well (that's a form of martial arts... he's a bit of a bad ass). That was by far the BEST massage I've ever gotten in life. Afterwards we finally made it back to his home and I put that CD in my personal CD player and kept it still with the album on repeat (it had to stay still because of our old CD players may or may not have had the anti-skip button, I don't think mine did). The album played and it was a great album from front to back. Then the last song played, this one was produced by J Dilla. You hear the horn play then the beat comes in followed by Bilal vocals. Common starts rapping.

"Went to school in Baton Rouge for a couple of years
My college career got down with a couple of peers.
Came back home, now I gotta pay back loans.
Same niggas, same block
Same shit they on.
Only thing different quicker, they click that chrome.
In my defense, yeah I had to hit that zone.
Man to man, I'm good working with my hands.
My generation never understood working for the man.
And… up being broke I ain't a fan.
Now I stand in the same spot as my old man.
My life I plan not to be on this corner,
I still wanna see California.
But this is my world."

This was again like seeing at a negative before it happened. I was on the way to college the next semester so I knew it was do or die. If I don't make it in college, I'll be dropping out, heading right back home with the same dudes I know that weren't doing better with their lives, owing money to a school that would show no remorse whether I was there or not and possibly just doing worse in life. I let Murphy know I got accepted into college at Prairie View A&M University but I didn't want to go. I didn't really want to go back to Texas after that heartbreak. In a gentle yet strong way, he let me know to get off the bullshit, life happens and you got to happen with it. Things aren't always going to go as expected but there were two things he let me know I needed. One, I needed to always keep moving forward no matter what life deals you, and two, I needed a nice pair of corduroys (weird, I know). So with the song playing, I must've played it about 53 times before I went to sleep. Why? At the end of the song (and album) there was a message played after you heard the song fade out with voices of a lot of kids speaking life into their dreams. "I want to be doctor.… I want to be a nurse… I want to be a police officer.… I want to be an artist… I want to be the first African American President of the United States.… I want to be a superstar! Then you hear the deep voice of a poet speaking what to be like:

"Be a map maker…

Be that… be this…

Be five fifths human… "

But mostly what stood out of what all he said in the long message at the end was "Be on time with nowhere to go". I thought to myself like "Hmm… so even if I have no destination, I still have to be present and ready when opportunity presents itself" (at least that's what I got out of it). Right then, I knew I was ready to return back home and whatever trials may come my way, I was going to be prepared for it. Even if I had no idea where I was going, I was going to make sure to at least be there. That's how I've been approaching life ever since. Opportunities come and go, but it's what you do with them when they come is what matters. Are you on time for an opportunity or are you late, still unprepared for what may be? Wise words spoken by many of dumb people states, "If you stay ready, you ain't gotta get ready" and as country and cliché it sounds, just think on that message on preparation. It may help you out too from day to day.

With Chrissy Depauw, the song "Chance" is something I've heard back in like 2008 in the last glory days of what some may call "Myspace" (an old website you probably would NEVER use). The singer was some white girl from California and at the time I was imagining if I had my own record label, what kind of mixture of artists I would have. This singer in particular stuck out to me when I found her at random. With only one song posted on her page at the time, I decided to give it a listen and it was a beautiful tune.

The song starts:

"Everybody thinks, if it's meant to be then it's going to be
Nobody starts to think, its might just be hard.
If good things come to those who wait
Then what do you get if you wait too late,
Nobody starts to think quite that far."

This alone made me think of opportunities of success. Sometimes you might expect things to go your way and then boop! Next thing you know you're in a pile of shit wondering how you got there in the first place. I'll go ahead and tell you, life is NEVER 100% what you expect. You might be expecting a daughter after 9 months of pregnancy and then surprise! It's a boy! You might be expecting to get a raise after 6 months working a job and then surprise! You're laid off with no eligibility of collecting an unemployment check. You might even come home to propose to your girlfriend of 3 years and then surprise! She's swallowing another man in your favorite "love" seat. Life happens, and like my cousin said, sometimes you got to happen with it.

Life's journey into what we want for ourselves is never a road built easy, no matter what circumstance. Athletes have to train hard through pain to get better at their skill. Lawyers have to study almost day and night to have to win cases that very well may change the shift of someone's life forever. Nurses have to work long hours to save the lives of women, men and children every day. It's all in order to one day say we've done something positive to change the world and that may very well determine your success. What you may determine as success one day to you may perhaps change. It may end up being different from someone else's measure of success and that's okay because you will always have your own scale of what you decide to measure success on. Will it be getting married and raising healthy kids? Will it be becoming a millionaire? Will it be traveling to see and check off every country in Africa? What will determine your level of success really? Then think of what it's going to take to accomplish that. "What will I have to do?" you might wonder. "How long is long enough?" "Will it be hard?" I'll tell you right now, most things that seem bigger than you may seem hard until it's done. But don't wait too long, that's where you'll build a deep pool of what feels like regret and that's an aftertaste no one really loves to enjoy once an opportunity is gone.

You might learn later in life the game of procrastination and how it can one day bite you in the ass. I've waited too long to do something I know I should have many times. Mainly with written assignments for college papers, I waited until the week of the due date or sometimes the day before to actually work on it. There have been times where I got lucky and the date was extended and there were times I just missed the deadline and got a zero. That responsibility kind of hits you different when you're on your own in college without parents around to check on you and make sure you did all your homework on time. So, like the quote from earlier, "be on time with nowhere to go." That's how you start to shift in life and create better opportunities by being first and not last, being ahead of the rest. And that's what I started to do with my life, I started being early more with everything. My assignments, my appointments, my interviews, everything! It's paid off for sure. Hell, I even had to take the chance on shooting my shot at your mom. To me, it was early. To her, it was on time. I had no idea she was finalizing a divorce and dating two other guys when I first messaged her. Please believe I was nervous enough to ask to get to know more of whom she was when I first spoke but little did I know, by taking that chance at that moment I took attention from any and everyone else she would speak with just so she could focus more on little old me. Life works like that and sometimes it's best to just take that chance.

With Musiq Soulchild's song "GiveMoreLove" from the album titled "Soulstar", this was the highlight and perfect way to end my favorite album of this artist. Musiq Soulchild to me was my personal introduction of what Neo-Soul music is. It's like Soul music with a new vibe to it that made it sound updated and more easily connected with my generation known as the "Millennials" (you'll hear a lot of things blamed on our generation but we're awesome!). But this song was sung so beautifully with such a positive message about love. I believe deep down my mind yearns for that and so does my heart so when I listen to both and come across music like this, I feel more at ease than I do with other music. Everything just tends to be alright. The message in this song starts:

"The children need something with more substance and more meaning.
The message intended to leave them with something much more to believe in.
Now it's to cool for us to say all the things we say and do
All the things we do to express ourselves
But we should try to find some way to bring balance to this hate
And leave a good impression on someone else.
Cause in our world...

There isn't much love going around
We should try to give a little bit more."

If you ask me, this song couldn't have started with a more honest observation of my generation. I feel we've been longing for something that's been more in reach to the audible ear to gravitate towards messages that didn't have to do with taking someone else's bitch, taking drugs till we die and making it rain late payments until we're flooded in debt. I mean Musiq Soulchild sung out a specific plan of what to do step by step, but his song was really enough of a message to give a first great step and that was to give more love. Love is the balance to what exists in hate. In fact, it took me years to understand that you would not be able to define love without understanding the definition of hate. That goes for the same with the concepts of good vs. bad, right vs. wrong, and God vs. the Devil. Son, we have so much hate in this world, it's unbearable.

If I didn't apologize for bringing you into this world, I apologize. But you're here now and it's a reason why you are that I'm not sure of and you have a better chance of finding out why than I do. But if you ever by chance feel like you didn't ask to be here and want to take it out on me or your mom, please try not to. I've been in your shoes and like I said, you're here for a reason I'm not able to explain. If you do so believe in a higher power, I suggest you ask for knowledge on what that purpose is and ask for the strength to perform whatever tasks may be and the guidance to show you the right way. Now like the song also states, it's cool to say and do what we do how we do, but we must have balance.

Freedom of expression is what has gotten humans to evolve to the advancement of a people today, and we're only moving forward. With the growth of that freedom of expression and so many mixed feelings, it is also easy to get caught in the mix of it all or as today we'd say "lost in the sauce". Doing good for the next stranger no matter what gets you farther in life than revenge on a known enemy. Good always trumps evil. Remember that. I could never love you son any less than I ever will because I know my love for you is unconditional. That's what I was taught about the love of the Most High, and I will make sure to love in the same way so that you would know firsthand what love is and what it is to be loved. I know if I make sure to do my duty, I've done my part in helping the world become a better place by instilling that same power within you. The torch is in your hand. Love forward.

Fifty Shades of Black

This is the part where we sit and I grab the bag of cookies and you get the milk and we really discuss something serious you need to know moving forward. Like always, I told you that I would always be honest with you, remember? So here it goes, not only are you mine and your mother's baby, but you're also Nigerian. I know... I know... hold on! You're also Native American.....but wait, there's more! You're also Mexican too. Chill bro, I know this is a bit much, but you're also Ghanaian too. Shit I don't know how, but you just are... oh yeah and you're Black too. What you mean what is Black? Whew.....okay here we go.

First let me tell you that Black is Beautiful. Uncle Huey and the Panthers wouldn't have wanted me to tell you any other way. Black is a color. Black is a state of mind. Black is a cultural being of African descent. Black is an attitude. Black is a statement. Black is a crime. Black is a privilege. Black is an honor. Black is a power, a magical supernatural power only some are blessed and cursed with. Remember when I also told you nothing in life was easy and the road was hard, yeah multiply that times 365 and that's what Black is too. Now, you look like me, yet you look like your mom. Your mother is of Mexican descent and I am of African descent. You have my features but you have your mother's skin tone. Both your features and skin tone are strong, people already see that and notice the beauty that lies in you since day one. It's something about you that brings joy to people when they automatically see you. That's a joy. That's the same joy that gives people the equal amount of pain when you or someone like you ends up hurt because of someone hating your features and causing you the most harm possible. It happens and it happens a lot. I'm not sure of the day that it will stop, but it happens. It can happen to you. It can happen to me. It can happen to the brother or sister next to you. It's an everyday thing here in our country called America. Why? We just got haters my boy. I mean come on, look at you. Now look at me. Look at you. Now look at me. We just got it going on. Some people don't got it like us and they hate us because they ain't us. That's just simple and plain young scrapper. Remember that. I also told you about the hate in the world, and that's part of it. Don't worry, it doesn't make you any more or less special. Hate because of ignorance comes in many forms for many reasons. It could be because someone's sexual orientation, race, gender, mental state, or anything. I like to say, "as long as there are people doing their ying, there's always someone waiting to yang your ass." To simply exist is dangerous enough and that message is taught to you in almost anything. I might get a little slack because of it but I like to compare the idea of being Black to being mutants in the Marvel X-Men movies. Like Black people, mutants just live on the planet doing what they do causing no harm. Yes they are different than most and they have the abilities to do things many can't and that alone threatens some of the normal humans (those who aren't Black). So some of them decide to attack the mutants simply because they are different and they don't understand their world or even try to. That fictional story with characters is the non-fictional life of the everyday Black person. Being Black is like something you can throw away yet you'll never get rid of. Some Black people don't consider themselves Black at all or even until it's time to (and yes, there is a time to be Black and time to play incognito). You ever wonder why the food tastes different with certain seasonings? Because Black that's why. You ever wonder why you hear multiple car doors locking in the parking lot when you walk through? Because Black that's why. You ever wonder why particular dogs always bark at you when you walk past the yard? Because their dogs, that's what they do... especially if you're Black (don't mess with those German Shepherds). Look I'm just going to tell you the good and bad experiences I've had with being Black in America and this may give you the understanding of why I am the way I am and why I may seem like I may be protecting you too much. So what would you like first, the good or the bad experience? Ha! Trick question, they're all good experiences. You just may like one more than the other but here we go.

Alright so in my first school ever named Stovall Elementary, Black students were the majority. We lived in the "subpar" good part of the hood in Acres Home, north of Houston. I was there long enough to get in trouble and I still to this day remember some of the kids in my classes like Jamarcus and Marcus, Chris, Robert, Ashley, Savannah and Lee. They were my closest friends then. We stayed laughing with each other and getting into shenanigans with the teachers but enough to stay learning yet entertained. I even learned my first important lesson in life and that was to always respect Black women. I'll tell you a funny story as to how I learned that.

I had this "girlfriend" back then, she was my first one ever. Her name was Cornelia, ugly name but a pretty girl. She was a tomboy. She was tough and could hang with the boys any day of the week. It was one day during recess we were playing dodgeball outside. Needless to say I was pretty damn good at it too. A ball was thrown in my direction and "Ahhh", just like that I'd shake it off quick enough to not get hit. I don't know where my strength came from that day but I threw the ball and hit this one kid in the face. I didn't do it on purpose but I was of course trying to hit him, not hurt him. Either way it goes, he didn't like that shit. So he came rushing towards my direction, kicking the ball far out in the field. Cornelia comes out of nowhere and pushed the boy down and starts yelling at him "You better leave him alone!" and this and that! I never saw anything like that before. I mean she came in with the strength of God and protected me. That was some next level shit right there and sure enough, the boy left me alone because he didn't want to see them hands. Not my hands, I mean hers. She could fight too. I wouldn't dare try to cross her. She pulled me to the side on the way to go get the ball from out the field and hyped me up saying stuff like "Ain't nobody gonna mess with you! Shoot, they got me messed up!" I was like "Damn right! I don't know what's wrong with these people." I had no clue on how to fight other than watching Jackie Chan movies, but I knew this Black girl had my back and I could never call another one weak from that day forward. But her along with my other friends felt like another branch of family, cousins if you will.

Then, my family decided to move. It was a hard bombshell for me because I didn't want to experience anything new. I just was getting along with the friends I did have and like I said, we felt like family. Moving tore me apart and wherever we were going, I knew in my mind I wasn't prepared to like it any kind of way. So we moved to a new home in the Cypress area of Houston, more northwest. Back then, it was way less Black people in the area and the ones around, you basically knew who they were. Let's just say if all the Black people in the area were in the phone book, we'd probably have one page with all of us written on the back. I was the only Black kid in my class from 3rd grade all the way to 7th grade. It was some of the most uncomfortable years. But I will say, even with that feeling against me seeming as if I was all alone in the world. I remember my first teacher who made a difference in my life, Mr. Solbeck. He couldn't deny my blackness although he was a tall, white man (my first male teacher at that) and I was the shortest one in the class. Mr. Solbeck saw something in me though, he saw intelligence.

In his 4th grade English class, we had weekly spelling tests, I always got A's if not 100% on the tests. He saw I was smart and nicknamed me "No Doubt Dowdy" because he knew I was going to get all the answers right. That made me feel good because for some odd reason, all the other students (being white) weren't doing that good at the spelling tests. Now let's pause for a second. The type of white people, who basically tried to deny Black people for years the education of even learning English, were in my English class failing at a language my ancestors weren't even able to learn, and I was there making A's on my tests? I'm not going to say I was cocky, but I was damn sure of myself that I wasn't dumb or I didn't belong, even if I was the only one that looked like me. That year I won the Spelling Bee at my school. I was hella proud of myself and at that moment, I knew my Blackness was a gift that not only separated me from my peers at the time but also made me shine in a way I never had before.

In 7th grade, there was another Black kid in my Math class named Jeremy (your play uncle). He looked similar to me, not exact but he was the same brown skin tone and height and many of the white kids got us mixed up thinking that we looked alike. We liked to fuck with their minds and tell them that we were really cousins and they believed us. That lie alone brought us together because we both knew that there weren't many that looked like us, and for how similar we were, we just might have been cousins and never knew. With us together our Blackness started to shine. We'd make jokes that only we would understand, almost like a code in a way. Next thing you know, there was a new student in our class named

Keith. He was a lighter skinned Black student from out of state. To keep him in the loop of what we had going on, we told the other white students that he was our cousin too (I think at that point, they were onto us). But all became close, we acted like cousins and protected each other and looked out for one another like family. At moments like those, being Black seems like an understanding, knowing that you're different and can be treated as such but taking responsibility for one another because you know the world can be shady and you just don't want to go through it alone.

Fast forward to high school and at this point it seemed like more and more Black students had moved into what "was" known as a white area over the past 6 years. My 9th grade was so damn lit, you couldn't pull us Black people apart. At this point we're about over 100 deep in a school with a little under 2000 students. 100 students don't seem that big of a number until you got us all in one room. Every morning before first period, that cafeteria was "our" room. We all would meet up and laugh, freestyle over beats, flirt with the girls and just spend time together. Every day was like a family reunion and we were glad to just spend time with people like us who understood each other without having to explain how we are as a people. This was beginning to be what I've longed for as far as school interaction among people like me but then the next year, it all changed. First day of 10th grade came and we all come to find out our school was "too high in capacity" and another high school was built across the freeway. Our high school attendance was split and zoned and the neighborhoods with more Black students in the area were split and were to go to the other school, Cy-Falls. My neighborhood (of course) was one of the ones that were going to continue going to my school, Cy-Fair (if that wasn't a pun within names). So more than half of the friends I had (including the ones I got in trouble with) were now gone. Looking back, that was probably a good thing, but didn't keep me out of trouble at all. Then the ultimate day came where things changed forever.

I had 2nd period English class and I was the first of my Black friends to have this class early in the day. In class, my teacher introduced a new book to the class that we were going to read. This book was called "To Kill a Mockingbird" (which the title, very fitting, had so much meaning to how I felt as a people). The teacher stated that we'd be reading this book aloud in class. As she was giving more details about the book, I became deafer to the sounds of the room as I was skimming through the pages of the book and reading the offensive words I saw. "Nigger this... nigger that... and blah, blah, blah, nigger. I haven't seen the word nigger written down so many times in my life. By now, you may know what this means son, but if not, let me explain. "Nigger" (emphasis on the "er") is a term meaning ignorant Black person or in likes of better terms someone Black that gets no love or respect. I KNEW in my mind and heart that this wasn't what I was. I knew I was smart. I knew I was not ignorant. I knew I was loved. But somehow just hearing that word over and over used in a room full of white people just made me uncomfortable like a motherfucker. I don't know why I didn't stop the teacher. I guess I just wanted to see how things would turn out. So the class started reading, each student reading a paragraph and going to the next student and then the next. The first student that came to the word "nigger" was an Asian girl. She kindly skipped the word knowing it was wrong to say and kept reading. I had to respect that because she didn't have to do that but she did and it said a lot about her and how she was raised. Then the second time the word was mentioned, it came to a white boy to read it out loud. When I tell you this dude read "nigger" louder than any other word in that paragraph, my blood ran hot in that room. I was pissed but I was in a way embarrassed because I felt that this was how some of the white people in the world thought and now it was being said out loud, in my own classroom. When he said it, I just kept reading looking down in my book shaking my head. I didn't want to look up because you could feel the heat from everyone's eyes looking at me. But as I raised my eyes to look at everyone else, I could see their eyes quickly looking nervously away from me. I knew that most of them were more embarrassed than I was ironically. But as soon as class ended, I walked quickly to meet up with other Black friends and asked them if they had been to English yet and they all said no. I told them "Aye, when yall get out of English, we gonna talk about what we're gonna do about this". They all sounded confused as to what I was talking about and I repeated myself (which I really hate to do). I didn't want to explain because I just didn't really know how to put my feelings in words. I just knew I was mad and I knew they would be mad too and something bad would happen because of it.

So later after all the lunches passed mid-day after 5th period, we all met up and had a heated conversation in disbelief.

"Yo' I can't believe we reading this shit!" my friend Ryan said.

"Somebody getting fucked up for this", Kevin replied.

All my Black friends we had left at this school were in total shock that this book was even in our curriculum to read, out loud at that! Even the Mexican friends we all had felt the same, even felt sad that we had to go through with that at all. Day by day goes by and the white students begin to change. They start wearing more cowboy gear often, redneck apparel, confederate flag stickers on the clothes, binders and trucks. They just started to wear their true colors. What sucked was that some of the white friends I "thought" I had started to switch up and you got to see them for who they really were. Black students started to get threatened of attacks left and right. A rope was hung outside one of my friend's house and he came back to school the next day and hit the first white person that even looked racist right in the face.

Another good friend of mine, Cordale, was what you would say the leader of a lot of us. When he said it's going down, you were there! He fought some big redneck, racist, white boy for calling him a nigger after school. The white boy hit Cordale so hard I thought the fight was going to be over. Shit sounded like a clap, but it was a punch! I would have been done for but not Cordale. He took that jab like it was nothing and just kept whooping that white kid's ass. It was terrible to see it all go down but it was a fight for respect is what I saw, and Cordale needed his respect.

I don't want to advocate fighting for any reason son, but what I will say is this. Sometimes you may have to protect yourself and one day you might very well get into a fight.

But no… not your dad.

I wasn't for the bullshit ever! I haven't gotten into a fight my whole life and not that I was scared but because I was fortunate. Every time someone wanted to fight me, one of my friends were always there to stand up for me, (although I never asked) it was just a respect thing people had for me. Hopefully you will have just as good enough people around you to keep you protected throughout life. But make sure they are people that would ride for you, no matter the outcome. Funny story, I was heading home off the late bus from school and I turn the corner on the way to the house and as I walk down the street, I see about three trucks outside the last house before you turn the corner to get to my street. Right outside that house, I see about fifty eleven white redneck kids hanging outside. As I'm walking in their direction one of them point at me. I thought that day I was going to get hung, beaten or something bad, just that Black instinct I guess. But when I tell you I ran faster than I probably ever ran in my life, I might have beaten all the Cantu brothers that day.

I ran to the nearest friend Jeffrey's house. I told him what was going on and he grabbed a bat and walked with me down towards my house. He saw the trucks outside, shook his head and said "Oh hell naw fam!" and he turned me around and we went right back to his house where we stayed for hours until they left. Moral of the story, make sure to pick your battles and don't let your battles pick you. People will be ready to attack you, slander your name, turn you down for opportunities, hate on you, and even worse kill you any day of the week. But you want to know the best part about it all? You can and will rise above it all! You're my son and if there's anything you don't understand, you will always have me to help you. Again, I can't stress this enough, I'm not perfect and I don't know everything but I've been on this earth longer than you and I've been Blacker longer than you've been talking so I know a thing or two that can help you and I both along the way. My job is to always be present in your life because sad to say, a lot of Black youth don't have the luxury of being raised by a father or even knowing who their father is. I need you to grow with a different kind of luxury of having access to the knowledge I have to give. Most people are betting on you in the future to not have that and be the "nigger" they may see in their eyes. But that's not you. You are royalty! You are destined for great things but again, you have to move forward on YOUR journey towards your path that is destined for you and you only. Just remember Black is your power. And I know you're probably wondering "What about your Mexican side?" Like I said, I don't know everything but I do know I know more Spanish than your mother. So in case in the future you get stuck at the border of Mexico, just make sure to say "Yo tengo el gato en los pantalones!" Works everytime! Just ask Martin Lawrence.

The Blueprint

As we talk now through this book, this is probably the most important lesson that you're going to learn in this chapter, so take a moment and get some more cookies as I tell you about growing up with my dad.

Now I first want to tell you that your grandfather is a loving, caring human being and like us all, we all have our faults. I love him still and he loves his children. Remember that time (probably not) when we were home, just the two of us, and you wouldn't stop crying so I just yelled at you to stop? We both know that didn't work and you started to cry even more. I just chose the last resort I knew which was just more love so I picked you up and held you close on my shoulder and just started rocking you. You stopped crying instantly and that's when I first knew you just needed love. Luckily, I learned that as you were a newborn and not later in life. That's where I feel my dad had learned, later.

Your papa was the oldest child of most of his siblings and he came from a split family. His mom and dad weren't together anymore and he grew up with his mom and grandmother but without his father. He had to learn parenting a different way, not to mention this was like the 1940's (by the time you'll read this he'll seem like a dinosaur to you). I remember he told me how he grew up and it wasn't the best for him but he learned what he learned and moved forward with the knowledge he was given. He went to the military and joined the Air Force where he was in the Vietnam War. This war left him with traces of Agent Orange, a known chemical used in the war that can leave terrible effects on your body over time and sometimes instantly. To this day, he is the only American awarded by the President of Vietnam with a Purple Heart for that war, which isn't normal for citizens to get awarded by the country you're fighting against. He's a bad ass but he doesn't like talking about the war and what he's done during it. I remember I asked if he ever killed anyone and he just got silent and then spoke "I don't want to talk about that period." I left it alone because I understood some things are just better left unsaid. My dad has this look on his face that says a thousand words without any being spoken. Your mother says the same about me so it's hard for me to hide anything I feel inside because she knows when something is on my mind or something is bothering me. Then I recognized and took a look at my history and noticed my dad's last name wasn't the same as his mother's or his father's. "Dowdy" is the last name that was taken from my dad's mother's second husband. His mother's last name was Fergerson and his father's last name was House. But later in life my dad met his biological father for the first time right before your Mimi gave birth to me. So between 1945 and 1987, my dad had to go through life without having a father and the knowledge one can give him to guide him in the right directions. That's 42 years my guy! That is a long time to take in consideration the effect of what that can do to a young man, especially in a time period when things were not the same as they were for you or even me.

I have to remember that. You have to remember that.

It wasn't until I was like 10 years old until I met my dad's biological father. He looked just like him and it was like looking at two of me in the future, but not. To this day I still don't want my last name after knowing how I got my last name and how it doesn't even follow the lineage of my actual bloodline. I understood how and why it happened the way it did for my dad, but I didn't like how it left me at the end of it all. I wanted to change my name to Shawn Joseph Fergerson (which sounds like an official author name now that I think of it). Part of me still wants to change my name and part of me wants to leave it as it is so I can still remember the how and why I got here. Hell you might even want to change your name later in life. Your mother and I named you Basquiat D'Angelo Xavier Dowdy. Basquiat was after the most famous Black American Haitian artist, Jean Michel Basquiat. D'Angelo was after the soul singer in the 1990's. Xavier was after two things, because Charles Xavier was one of my favorite characters in the cartoon X-Men and the X was symbolization of Malcolm X, one of mine and your mother's favorite History subjects to study from the 20th Century. So now that you know, I hope you're at least happy and comfortable with your name. I used to not like my first name, Peter. I thought it sounded too white, but that's because I didn't know any Black people with my name and I've only heard on TV characters with that name were white. I conditioned myself to not like it. But now that I'm older, I've found a new appreciation for my name and its uniqueness (plus your mom makes it sound pretty good). I mean, after all it was the name that my dad gave to me. I just somehow wonder why he named me after a guy who denied he knew a guy named Jesus multiple times in the Bible that he was always hanging with……ohhhhhhh….. Now I think I know. Because if I was always with my boy Kris and the cops came to me on some crazy shit like they were going to kill me for being involved with him for some crime, I would act like I didn't know him either. Call me a hoe, but that's who your dad is. I can't take the L for anybody, especially if it costs my life. Then who would take care of you for the next 42 years huh? Yeah, exactly!

But that's just how my dad grew up. I, of course, grew up differently than him. With both of my parents in the household, things you can say were better than most without. My dad was always at work at the post office with like 14 different hustles or side jobs and my mom had one solid job, first at the UT in the medical center and then at Continental Airlines. What got my dad hustling so many jobs and skills was his growing up. That's all he knew was to get it on his own and work hard no matter what, whether for himself or working for someone else. That hustle never stopped and only went harder right after I was born because both my parents were laid off and left with no place to live and no jobs. I remember we moved in your Aunt June's house, which was your great-grandmother's house on my mom's side. Although I never met my grandma, I heard she would have loved me just as much as my mom loves you. But like how my mom's parents got divorced, I thought it would be the same with my parents as well. With so much arguing in the house, I really thought it was just a matter of time. Either it was over someone not listening, someone misunderstanding, or money issues. These problems alone I take heed to recognize its power and the power to control these traits in ways where one could have a better marriage with better problems, because again, you'll never, NOT have problems. Looking back now, I see how stress and changes of events in life, social activity, employment and stability can play a role in a steady peace within a household and family.

Later down the line, when my parents got another stable home, it seemed as if I only remember seeing my dad on the weekends. He always worked at night and during the day he would sleep. Maybe during the day he would be working on his insurance business or some other lucrative pyramid scheme program he had going on just to make any kind of extra money. We'd see him during dinner before leaving for work because he would always be the one to cook (being a chef was one of the other hustles). On the weekends, he'd be at the barbershop cutting hair or working at his shoe shine and repair stand. He was about getting the dollar not for just his own personal gain, but to take care of his family by any means. I knew that so I would feel that I would understand more than my sisters because I'm a man (or was growing to be one) and I knew I would have responsibilities as such one day. The most time we'd spend together was Sunday's, where of course, he was a minister and Pastor at times. This wasn't a time for him to work for monetary gain, but this was a time for him to serve out of thanks for all that he HAD been able to receive to take care of us. I look back at that now and understand it more clearly. But as much as he was gone, sometimes I wish he was around more or at least felt like he could afford to. I kind of didn't take up too many extra-curriculum classes in school because I felt like my parents wouldn't be there for any major events. The only thing I was in was choir and when it came to recitals or concerts, I know my dad never came because he was either catching up on sleep or already at work. My mom really even only came three times, once in middle school and twice in high school. My mom was the one parent who understood me most emotionally and I could always talk with her in ways I felt like I couldn't with my dad. Most of the talks with my dad was me getting yelled at or him knowing what's best for me and not really asking me what I think. Not much compassion came from my dad as much as my mom and I felt that for a very long time. For example, my best friend Cordale (they kid who got punched in the face at school) had died during my freshman year of college after being shot by a cop in the back of the head during a robbery. I called my mom to get some healing over the phone, you know just to hear some kind words to assure me things were going to be alright. She answered and spoke to me, which made me feel a little better but before I got off the phone I hear her say "Hold on, here's your dad." That's not at all what I wanted to hear because I knew I wasn't going to get that same kind of compassion that I received from my mom. By the time he got on the phone, I had to tell him everything that happened again and as I started crying on the phone, all I could hear him say first was "Well I told you about the wrong people you hang around..." As true as that statement was, it made it worse because that's definitely not what I personally needed to hear at that moment. Sometimes, even being right could come at the wrong time and my dad never really understood that. But this was my life. These were my parents and although they both had to provide for me and my sister in the house the best they could, my dad worked the hardest outside of the house.

But where his job at the post office weighed on him year after year, mentally and physically, some of that pain he would take in would be brought home only to share with the rest of us and not in the best way. He would mostly find a reason to yell because something wasn't taken care of at home or cleaned properly. Well it really could be multiple reasons, but whatever the reason, if my mom wasn't getting yelled at, either I or my sister Kristen was getting yelled at. But our childhood wasn't all beating and just yelling, yes it was enough of it, but there was also love, strong love, but love regardless. There were two times I couldn't walk for some odd reason, once at eight years old and another time when I was sixteen. I remember my teenage years more prevalent because I was home alone. I couldn't stretch my legs and was basically paralyzed on the ground for two hours before my dad came home. Old and still with enough strength, he picked me up and carried me all the way to the car and took me to the hospital. I walked again after three days (could you believe it was just locked up gas in my butt?). His strength in that moment carries a lot with me in life because I saw effort to make sure to be there no matter what and how in that moment in life.

As more time passed, I got a little older and he got a little older and sicker. My dad's health wasn't always the best but it's gotten him here today to still be standing. I have looked back at the beginning of his life and how it relates to mine and what I've realized is:

-stability matters

-peace matters

-love matters

-understanding matters

-compassion matters

These factors are what my family particularly lacked at times and those times created a huge effect on the growth of the child (myself) over time. On the other hand, the knowledge of this alone helps to pinpoint what about me needs to be present for my own household to raise you the right way. The last thing I want is for you to see your mother and I arguing. It's not normal no matter what people say. It's not productive in any way. Most importantly, it's not right.

I've learned how to love by learning how not to love. I hope that makes sense to you, if not just read that sentence again. What was missing, I've found those pieces and I'm just learning how to put them in place in this puzzle we call a relationship. In fact, I don't know what I'm doing but I do know what I'm not doing and that is good enough to keep an understanding and compassion for one another between your mother and I to raise you with the best example we know how to be. I'm always going to be on the go and that's why I want you by my side every step of the way. You'll learn from my achievements as well as my downfalls. I've missed most of those moments with my dad by choice and I hope you won't repeat the same mistake I made. My dad hasn't always been the best with raising me but he's been the best at providing, and that's where I get my hustle from. So with grandfathers and grandchildren, the bridge of missed opportunity comes together to pick up where one left off and get things right on a brand new slate. You are my dad's second chance and every grandpa deserves another try.

You Can Have Your Cake and Eat It Too

You're almost 1 year old now. Wow! Time has passed by pretty quick since you've been born. You're walking now, feeding yourself like a champ, and even singing out loud almost everywhere. Your mom tells me you're a character and I can't wait to get back to see you and hug you. This job that I'm on now isn't that much of a struggle but it's a better struggle than I've had before. You wouldn't believe all the things I've experienced on the way to even knowing more of who I am as a person before even meeting your mother. I was a wreck! A careless, selfish individual that would get what I want by any means at the expense of anything or anyone. Aunt Karma never forgets that either and she made sure I'm well taken care of for the things I've done, good and bad. That's also why I had to make changes in my life for the better so that I could have better problems. I had to learn that they don't go away.

If you hit the lottery the first day you turn 18, you can expect I'm going to hound you to make sure you don't waste it all (without getting a piece). If you got dumped by your significant other, you have to think if you want another relationship and with who? If you got sick, you have to be cautious on any medicine you take that's not natural and even then you have to find the right remedy before you get worse. Problems are going to be there and the struggles are the process of making them better. With knowing that, there are four points I want you to take with you in life:

-Learn from mistakes, yours and others (other people's mistakes are the best kind to learn from)

- Be prepared to make a way out of no way

- Tough times don't last, tough people do

-Starting over is okay

These four points should help guide you to move forward with thinking to get past whatever issue you may be dealing with. This is what worked for me and it may very well work for you as well. This might even help guide you to find even better solutions for the problems that you will have, but this is the knowledge I wanted to give to you. I owe myself the responsibility to provide you with this knowledge for when you do struggle.

Embrace those struggles because that is what will define your integrity, strength, courage, hustle, and basically your whole personality afterwards. How well you handle a situation can make you a more dependable person. That doesn't mean you're making yourself better for someone to use you. But you might have the knowledge someone else needs one day to help them along. It won't hurt for you to share that knowledge no more than it hurts me to write this book, and this doesn't hurt a bit. So I'll share with you a bit of my struggles so that way you know more of how I am and what obstacles I had to overcome to get to where I am now. Although even now I'm not where I want to be, I'm not where I used to be either by far.

Back in freshman year of college, I had this Sony laptop computer that my dad bought me. This computer was very thick and had a lot of space enough for me to save lots of drawings since I was taking Architecture classes. But I didn't save my drawings on there, at least not much. I had more music than anything else on that laptop. The more music I added to the computer, the slower it ran. I didn't care. Album after album and song after song, I just kept adding away until I couldn't think of anymore songs I wanted. The last thing I can remember I downloaded was Drake's mixtape So Far Gone. Ironically after that, so was my computer. It crashed on me in the middle of my semester and I was too ignorant on how to get it fixed right away and all my files on the computer were lost by the time I got it back working. I even had an extra hard drive but I didn't save everything on it. I eventually lost that hard drive later on some carelessness and not taking care of what was mine. That was a hard lesson in responsibility for my own property. Although that computer that crashed wasn't at its best state and I lost my hard drive, in order to not go through the same situation again I got two new portable hard drives. That way no matter where I go, I would have my files saved on the hard drives as well as a back-up one no matter what computer I used. Take my situation and learn from it so you will be better prepared for your own mistakes to handle them with grace. This was my first lesson with my computer and learning how to manage working around issues that I've caused myself with the things I care about. With that, my lessons didn't stop there and my problems didn't go away.

I bought myself a new computer after saving up from working. This computer was smaller and easier to take everywhere I went. I made sure to get this kind because I knew the first one I had was hell to take around on campus and got overheated quicker because of its size, type and brand. So with my new computer I felt like the man. I had it all figured out, well at least I thought so. Now at this time, I was a pretty avid user of marijuana. I smoked almost all day and night in college. As soon as I woke up I smoked. I went to class, and then I smoked. I went to lunch, and then I smoked. On the way to work I smoked. After work, I smoked. Smoke, smoke, smoke, smoke, smoke! That was my life in my college days. Don't get me wrong, these times were some of the best of times and I've learned a lot and still remember what I've learned from smoking. But this one day, I really regret smoking at that time. I left campus and drove into the city for something I needed from the store for my computer. At that time, I also had a raggedy car my parents let me have. Raggedy might be a bad choice of words for an all-Black convertible 1993 Mercedes Benz CL300, BUT….it was given to me with a shady ass transmission, the radio and windows didn't work, it would overheat at random, it was a two door and two seater and it would mostly not work during cold weather (mind you they gave me this car during the winter). Now I was grateful because I did fuck off my first car which they gave to me too but this got me (sometimes) from A to B. I stopped after making my store run to put some water in the coolant tank for the car so it wouldn't overheat on me. As I stopped I took the time to roll up a blunt and … yes son you guessed it. I smoked. I hooked up the tape adapter to connect to my computer so I could listen to my music in the car while I drive. I must've gotten really high as hell because when I drove off, I got back on the freeway and I could hear honking. I kept hearing this noise but shrugged it off because you'll always hear someone's horn in Houston and it's not always meant for you. But I just so happen to look out the window to my left while I was smoking. This man driving next to me was honking and making an alligator mouth opening sign with his hands. I knew I was high but I thought this guy was higher because I didn't understand what he was doing until I heard a noise. All I could hear was "bump, bang, bop," and I looked in the rear view mirror but I didn't see anything. I looked down and didn't see my computer there. That's when I realized that guy was making a laptop closing sign, not an alligator.

Damn!!!

I never was good at playing charades, but I wish I was a champ then. I played myself hard. I got so high that I was forgetful enough to sit a laptop on top of my car and drive off like nothing could go wrong. That computer had to be crushed in pieces because I know I felt and heard those pieces on the freeway after driving back around. It was done for! I learned that I have to pick my times better to smoke and learn to be more aware of my surroundings when I do decide to get high. I also learned that I can also be the factor for holding myself back by making poor decisions like that. I'm not going to tell you not to smoke son because that'll be crazy. But I will say, be responsible for your own actions and hold yourself accountable when or if you do decide to partake. I'll teach you later about the differences of indica and sativa strains but that's for a later time (wink). Let's just say I wish I had sativa strains that day to help me focus more.

The lessons didn't even stop there with my computer experiences. At that time, I was with no computer in 2009, which was probably the worst year in my life that I remember (I almost died but I'll save that for another time). It was summer time and I was in a relationship with someone I was living with in Dallas. She got an apartment and I moved in with her and her daughter. WARNING: Never move in with anyone you're not married with or at least plan on marrying. I had no phone, no computer, and no job. I was a bum but let me tell it then, I was just figuring things out. I wasn't the best person I could be but something started to kick in to let me know that something had to change. I actually wanted more out of life, I just had to get off my ass and do something. I had to use the best thing I had available that I'd never run out of, and that's the thoughts in my mind. I wanted to work on music so bad and with no computer I had to figure out how I could. I started listening to music more closely, closer and closer. The more I envisioned music the more creative I got.

I started to draw what I heard, from the kicks, hi hats and snares, I heard it all so I drew them all. I made little boxes in the form of the beat pattern that the song would follow and color in the boxes where I heard each sound come in so I knew where it was placed on the beat. As I did this, I noticed I was basically creating beat loops through art so that way whenever I DID get another computer, I could make these same beat loops and put them on my own samples I used to make some great music. Then I did just that. I took all the beats I drew and created the loops and made music out of each one. That was the most creative I felt in a long time back then. I was without so much yet I found joy in what I did have and I made it work for me. This is what I want you to learn my boy. There's going to be times where you feel as if you were set back and taken back a few steps. Those are important times to reflect on the resources you already have and to utilize that to the max so that way when you do have the opportunity to get more out of life, you can better appreciate the small things and capitalize on the bigger things later.

Things got better as time passed but yet again my computer went out on me. I know you're probably thinking "Man, how bad are computers and will I have the same problem?" It's possible but I also have faith in the future by the time you have your own personal computer, technology will have advanced in ways to avoid the crashing and wear and tear that computers have been used to over the past few years for me. But I was in need of a computer and this time I didn't have the funds available to just up and get a new one instantly. My sister just so happened to have an extra mini laptop that she wasn't using. It had a cracked screen but I told her I could make it work. And that I did! I had an extra computer screen I found somewhere and I hooked up the laptop she gave me to the screen so I could see. It was a janky set up but I managed to get a lot accomplished. I used to write papers for other students in college this way to make extra money. I did my own homework online with this set up. I even went to the music studio where I met up with all my college friends to work on various projects and made music with this set up. My friends would be amazed at how I could even make beats on the laptop without the screen hooked up as if I was some kind of music genius. They made me feel like I was, and maybe I was. But really, I was just heavily determined to work and create with what I had no matter what. I wasn't going to let me losing a hard drive stop my grind. I wasn't going to let my high tendencies and damaging my computer stop me. I wasn't going to let having no computer at all stop me. And I sure wasn't going to let having a cracked screen stop me from working. I was determined and I still am.

Music is one thing I have been good at that I have yet to quit. It's my own sport that I feel comfortable with. I practice every now and then, sometimes a little less than when I had nothing but time in college, but I still practice to perfect my sound. It's what I love.

In my last year of college, with a cracked screen laptop I found myself homeless without a place of my own. I didn't want to stay with my parents because they were at least an hour and some change away from my school where I would have to drive that distance back and forth each day. Plus my relationship with my dad in that household wasn't always the best. So with my hard head ways and a mind and heart full of determination, I just finished my year out sleeping in my car. I had my blankets in the trunk along with my clothes for the week. I had old fast food bags lying on the floor and under the seats next to old pairs of socks. And if that wasn't bad, I had a glove compartment FULL of Taco Bell napkins to wipe my ass when I took a shit in the car. It was so uncomfortable and most people probably wouldn't live in the same conditions, but I did. This was my life and I was determined to finish school this time with nothing in my way to stop me. I was working two jobs and had twelve hours of school each week. This was a hard time for me, but I managed to find my peace through it all. Sometimes on the cold nights sleeping in the back seat, I would plug up my phone to the cigarette lighter which had my charger hooked up so I could also use it as my alarm to wake up on time for class. I would lie there and go online to Google Earth and just look at random places around the world and zoom in. This was my way of traveling. It was my inspiration to remind me that I wouldn't always be in that position I was in at the time and that I have more places to go and things to see. I would zoom into Africa, Australia, Europe, Asia, all the continents that I could, even Antarctica.

Then when I got hungry, I went online to Pinterest to look up recipes. I would see pictures of different dishes of food and would save the images. I would stare at these pictures long enough until I wasn't hungry anymore. It was like I would eat through my vision and get full after I scrolled and saw enough of what I needed to see. This was my way of survival and although it was a struggle, it was my struggle and I made the best of it. I just knew that when I finally got my own place and I was able to travel like I want, I would one day visit these places and eat these meals I saw online. I was living my dream through vision before I lived it in person. I still do this. Many people do this with vision boards, but I decide to go through it more in depth; especially during my struggles. I was able to finally graduate that year. Later I moved to a different city with a different car. After that, finally got my own place with your mother and life has been on the right track for me since then.

So just remember, continue to learn from your mistakes and remember these mistakes I told you about with me personally. This may help you in the future. Be prepared to make a way out of no way, you never know when hardships may come your way. Just make sure to have a little extra of what you need, not what you want. Know that tough times don't last, tough people do. Your struggles define your path in the direction you choose to move. Will you fall backwards and stay there or will you fall, dust yourself off and act like nobody seen you and move faster? Whatever happens, know that starting over is also okay. Things happen. Life happens. Just move with it. If you can manage to do the last three things mentioned, then starting over won't be shit to you because you know if you can do it once, then you can do it over and over again until you get it right. You will get it right! I believe in you, so just believe in yourself. You got this!

Fix It Yourself

With how things are in today's time in 2019, many people are leaning more towards to owning their own businesses rather than working eight or more hours at a job they may not like or need. It's a beautiful time to see more people looking forward to owning their own business. Although many people aren't fit to be an owner of a business, I know that you are. The way I see you grabbing for toys or food that isn't yours lets me know that you at least understand the concept of ownership. You'll probably beat my ass in Monopoly. But it's my job to best prepare you for the road to ownership the best way I know how. Just take note that I don't know everything but I feel I know enough from experience to tell you what worked and didn't work for me and you can take the bits and pieces from it that works for you.

Now my first taste of understanding owning my own business was in fifth grade. My elementary school was teaching us the idea of economics and the school came up with the idea to create a currency called "Lamkin Bucks". Lamkin was the elementary name so that answers the question you have as to why we called it that. We had to think of something to create that would be able to be sold and bought by other students. My choice was to make Rice Krispies treats, a snack baked with the Rice Krispies cereal and marshmallows. It was delicious! In fact, I made a lot of Lamkin Bucks at school. I didn't make the most, some student who made chocolate chip cookies made the most (which I should've known, that's my favorite snack as you may know). That was enough to teach me about customer needs, business competition, quality vs. quantity, costs and profit. Had I chosen a different product like chocolate chip cookies, I may have made more money. I would have also had to be conscious of the other girl who was selling cookies too. Would I have better tasting cookies? Would I have more available or enough? How much would I have spent making the product to sell and how much money I would make from products sold? These are basic questions you have to ask yourself when you have your own business and you have a product or service to sell. A more important question would be does your product or service solve a major problem that needs solving. If it doesn't, you need to switch to something that does solve a problem. That's a must!

I took that knowledge into every business I started over the years after. I saw a need for everything I did and solved a problem by providing a product or service at the right time. In the future, technology will be solving a lot of problems for humans and it will be your job to stay ahead of the curb of technology and find a solution for a problem that tech can't or hasn't solved yet. Remember this! The advancement of technology can take away your hustle or it can transform your hustle in a new way. For example, back in high school there were very few students who had CD burners. CD burners were used to duplicate any album you wanted. Back then, some people even had up to six, seven or eight tower CD burners where you could make more than one copy at a time.

This was a hustle I saw from one student named Kenneth. He was a young rapper along with his brother with the record label Rap A Lot records and he had access to having a multi- CD duplicator. This was very expensive and almost exclusive to even have, but he had it. So any CD you wanted, if you named it he would get it for you. If it was a real hot popular album that just came out, you can bet he already had plenty of copies of them and brought them to school to sell. That was his lick and I peeped it all and soaked up game. A demand was made for accessible music at a cheaper rate than what was sold in stores and Kenneth had a way to supply on that demand. It was basic economics to me; I just didn't have the access to what he had to do the same. When I graduated high school and went to college, it was a new ball game. It was many more students available with the same demand with a twist. People wanted a variety of music all on one disk to listen to in their downtime but sometimes had no way to get all the songs they wanted downloaded. I knew how to work around that. I downloaded music all the time and used file conversion websites to get the songs if they were harder to get online without purchase. I would ask people if they would like a personal mix CD made for them, and they would give me a list of songs. I would download them in class or out of class and I would burn them on a CD for them for about $5. I didn't have a personal CD burner so I used the computer in the library which did so I could have my service run that way. All my costs consisted of was buying the blank CDs and the jewel cases or sleeves to put the CD in for quality delivery. My cost generally cost about thirty dollars so I knew I only had to sell six CDs to break even with the amount of money I spent. If I wanted to double my money in what I spent for supplies, I figured I either had to sell twelve CDs or raise my price. So I did both. I could afford to because not many people provided the same service at all and the demand was still there. Now I could sell six CDs for $10 each and make double what I spent on costs. This was a smart move for me, but technology got smarter and so did my customers. As people generally started to learn how to do it themselves, CDs slowly became more obsolete and MP3 players were the new wave. Now people could save their music on a device to carry on the go and not have to worry about having so many CDs to carry. This was good for technology but bad for my business, so I had to move on to something new.

MP3 music became more accessible to download with the advancement of technology. More people started to use music apps like iTunes and SoundCloud. I had to switch up my hustle because people weren't buying CD mixes as much. With that knowledge I used my mind and thought of what else I had that I could use to make me extra money. As I walked back and forth to class each day, this thought would stick to my mind. A walk around campus, the park, or the neighborhood would normally get my mind going, but I noticed something particular on this one journey. As I looked around campus, I noticed that many students were walking around just like me. The number of cars that I saw in comparison to the number of students let me know that every student couldn't have possibly had a car; and if so, then many of them didn't have it on campus. I had my Saturn SL1 that my dad got me for my college car. It was already 10 years old but I didn't mind that at all. I was glad to have something that I could use to get me around. It wasn't the best of vehicles but it did get me moving and because of that I thought of using my car as a taxi service for other students who weren't fortunate enough to have a car. Crazy thing is during that time, companies like Lyft and Uber didn't exist yet but I was running my business on a small scale just like them. I'd advertise my new taxi service online and by word of mouth and next thing you know, the customers started rolling in. Our college was about 25 minutes from the outskirts of Northwest Houston. Remember I told you that saying, "Houston is an hour away from Houston"? You have a while to really understand but as much as the city is growing by the time you're old enough to drive, the distance and time may be longer. The students had lots of different places they needed to go. Some students were from out of town or state so when it came to the holidays, they needed a ride to the airport and I provided that. Some students needed a ride to the store to get groceries at the "good" Walmart in Houston and I provided that. Some students just needed a ride to the mall or to the Southside of Houston and guess what... I provided that too. Sometimes it was really convenient to take customers to where I needed to go as well because I may have been low on gas for the week or I needed to do something in Houston and didn't feel like wasting my gas to do so. It was a win for me to get paid to run my errands just by dropping someone else off. I normally just charged $20 for the whole ride, whether it was one way or round trip. This allowed for the opportunity for more than one person to ride along as well. I set my fees the way I wanted to for two reasons:

-because there wasn't any competition around

-more people in the car expands my network of connections

When you have a business and very little competition, you can afford to have a higher rate or standards set a certain way because you are providing a product or service that's hard to get. Plus, the more people you get to interact with your business also expands your clientele for future endeavors. For example, with all the services I've provided in my college years like this taxi service, essay writing service or even middle-man weed selling service, some of the people I've interacted with have been clients of the art business your mother and I have now. You'll never know how you'll get paid through your business in the future if you don't focus on building a business to get paid in the present.

When my junior year came, it was my most challenging year. My degree classes weren't getting any more interesting, I was becoming more unmotivated and if that wasn't enough, my school let me know that I had to pay almost $2,000 before

I could enroll into classes the next semester. With it being Fall semester receiving this news, I didn't know how I was going to get this money and this was making me depressed. I started to let my friends and roommates know that I may not come back to school the next semester. My roommates were your Uncle Kris, Justin and Morrel. Now Morrel was the wildest of us all. He's the reason why we called our dorm Club 1016, because we always had so many people at our spot. We didn't mind it because everyone who came over was cool. We'd play video games, talk shit, eat and smoke. Now I never smoked up to this point so let me explain how I started first, then I'll get back to the money. So, after I let the roommates know that I wasn't coming back. Morrel was like, "It's cool, I'm not coming back next semester either, but let's celebrate. I didn't know why not coming back to school became a celebration, but it did and I was cool with it. That was enough for me, plus what did I have to lose? Later that night, a few people came over and we were all drinking and having a good time. Morrel made a homemade bong for everyone to smoke out of. What's that? Well son it's basically this fire ass mechanism to smoke out of made with:

-an Ozarka bottle

-a cooking pot (preferably bigger than the bottle)

-aluminum foil

-a lighter

-water

-and of course, the weed

      Little did I know, this night was one I don't think I'll
ever forget. Morrel put the weed in the aluminum foil, lit it up
with the lighter and let the smoke gather inside the bottle and
then sucked all the smoke out. It was like some crazy science
project that everyone was enjoying. He said "You're up next"
as he lit another round. I wasn't scared but I was nervous
because this time the smoke got dark gray as he lit it up. I was
like "Who gone finish this with me?" Everybody at the same
time said "YOU". That's when I knew I was in trouble. I went
ahead and breathed all the smoke I could out the bottle and...
(coughs) whew... that was the most burning sensation I've
ever felt in my throat! My eyes teared up automatically and I
couldn't stop coughing. I opened the front door and threw up
a little right outside. I held my head up and smiled laughing for
some odd reason. Then what's crazier than that, I ran to my
car that wasn't even a running vehicle anymore. I sat in the
backseat of it and just kept laughing to myself for like ten
minutes. Just laughing at nothing. I honestly couldn't have
been happier.

I didn't care about any stress, no school, no depression, no worries at all. I was just happy, and maybe the happiest I've been in my life. This introduction to weed began my years of smoking to this day. That day made me also think to myself that this experience happens for a lot of college students. Many of us smoked during, in between and after classes and then experienced one of my favorite side effects, "the munchies". The munchies are just something you experience when you get high and have the cravings to eat a lot of food afterwards. With this as a common experience, the roommates and I all decided to go in together and start up a munchies store in our dorm room. We'd put some of our money together and Morrel would go to the store for us, get a lot of snacks and such. We'd change shifts when one of us had class or something to do and we'd stay open from early about 8 am till almost 1am. Our hours were set but some people didn't care, they'd still stop by whenever, whether it was after hours or not. We got many customers on a continuous basis and were able to make money and save some too, but then there was one day that changed our perspective. It was a random Saturday and Morrel was sleep in his bed. We all heard a noise of something breaking but didn't know what it was. Some random guy broke Morrel's window and started to try to come inside. Luckily Morrel was in the room and work up in time to scare the guy away. We all were high and laughing it off but in the back of our minds we knew we had to make some changes.

Although this business was profitable, the safety of ourselves and others we care about was a lot more important so we decided to end our operation. We even kept turning away customers after we shut the store down. That was the best decision we could have all came up with that week and truth be told, if I went back and did all of that again as an option, I'd choose to do it all again. No regrets. What I want you to mostly understand from this is to always be a step ahead of the game and stay intelligent enough to your mind to think of opportunities the make extra income, not only for yourself but for your family that you will have one day. Whether you're alone or in business with others, risks will come and great rewards can come from those risks. But stay smart my boy, if it feels like trouble is around the corner, take another route. There are so many problems out there to fix, and remember problems don't go away, they just become better. Become lucrative by making yours and others problems better.

Waterfall

For me growing up, I've seen men and boys told many things about feelings and emotions and how it's odd or not cool to show them. What's odd to me is how certain people are told to hold things in or not react in ways that would be normal for any other person. The main emotion you would see men holding back would be tears. I would understand how and why men do with the reasoning of some labeling them as weak individuals or sensitive and not really taking the time to understand where their tears come from. The connection with crying normally comes from pain, heartbreak or death and sometimes even joy and gratitude. I've seen people cry in church simply because they're thankful for God's blessings. I've seen homies cry over a lost friend. I've seen the homeless cry because of embarrassment. People cry for different reasons, but you should never be told not to show your emotions or hold them back for any reason.

That's one thing I would love to exercise with you as you get older. I wasn't taught the same unfortunately but as always, it's things I like to reverse from my experience through you to see those changes reap in better outcomes. I saw you cry for just a bit as you were taken out of your mom at birth (no you weren't dropped off by a stork, you were cut out of your mom's stomach). As I was first to hold you, you automatically stopped crying and I just spoke life into you as planned as soon as I held you. I wanted you to hear my voice but more importantly I wanted positive words to come through you for you to embody as I nurtured you the best way I could. I described you with adjectives, one for each letter in the alphabet. "You are amazing, you are beautiful, you are courageous, you are destined, you are enough, you are favored, you are greatness…" I wanted to hold you forever because I knew you wouldn't be that size for long. You were so small and precious. You're still precious but you're getting so big now. As you get older, you'll cry more for random things I'll try to understand. I won't get mad every time you cry and I have to remind myself of that. As the years go by, your tears will come and I have to be okay with that. Now I'm not wanting you to cry at every expense to get your way or what not, but I would like to take the time to understand your emotions, actually talk with you to see where your tears are coming from and what I can do to help change that or make you feel better. I believe it's that time invested in you or anyone for that matter that can make a big difference in making the world a better place if we all can take the time to view the understanding of one another.

My goal is not to parent you the way I was done in certain ways. I cried for many different reasons but mostly it was because I got whooped. My parents mainly whooped me with a belt, switch or the hand. Remember that belt I told you about that my dad had, that was like a finisher move type weapon. I like to call it a weapon because I felt defeated every time something like that was used to teach me any kind of lesson. My parents were big on the bible and there is a verse that reads, "Spare the rod, spoil a child". That means to some people if you don't whoop your kids, they will grow up to become spoiled or unappreciative. I never felt I was spoiled. Every time I asked for something I got a maybe or a no. I didn't want much and the things I got a yes for after asking, I didn't really want as much, I was just working through my law of averages with the nos. I would even be polite (because that's what I was taught by my parents) and say please, thank you, yes sir and no sir. That helped but not always. I could say please stop during a whooping, did it stop? Ha! Nope. Or another funny time, my sister and I like to joke about this because it's so real. When my dad whooped us, he was pretty consistent in his process. He would hit us on like every fuckin syllable of every word in a sentence and if he paused, that next hit was just him catching his breath and coming with more force. Typical. Then he would ask some stupid ass question like "Do you understand me!?" I'd be like "(cries) Yes sir…" and he would follow up with "I don't think you do" and keep whooping my ass. He did that almost every time and I never understood why, but you just knew it was fucked up but kind of funny later down the line. Like why would you ask someone a question and then say you don't think they understand when they answer quite sure? It was just stupid to me and after that, I knew if I'd ever have kids I didn't want to whoop them for one, especially if it didn't make sense. I'd feel my kids would be smarter than me and would call me out for doing something dumb like that. I'd be damned if you or any other kids point out how stupid I was. I can do that myself. Another time was being whooped for the wrong thing.

Okay so the story goes, I came home from school one day and went straight to my room. I knocked out my homework and then I hopped on my video game. That was my daily routine, I had to make sure my homework was done before any kind of entertainment. That's how it should be so expect at least me to be the same way with you. Then my dad came home and went to the kitchen, mind you I didn't go in the kitchen so I had no idea what was in there. He found a broken glass in the sink and thought I did it and just came to my room door yelling saying "I told yall about leaving dishes in the sink didn't I?" "Yes sir," I replied. "And now you got broken glass all in the sink and I gotta clean it up…" he said as he just walked off fast.

Now the walk away mid-sentence let me know he was going to get something. With my ass whooping experience, I already knew it was a belt. I wasn't prepared for this ass whooping. I didn't even have time to put on the extra pair of boxers and pairs of socks (because he like to hit low AND high). I was comfortable until he came home. Normally the sound of the Mercedes diesel engine pulling up was enough nervousness for me because I knew he was tired and busy so much that he was always yelling and mad for some reason other than just us at the house, so I just wondered most of the time "What could it be today?". After he came back with the belt it was over. I was now getting my ass whooped for something I didn't even know happened and it wasn't my fault. My mom called later and told him she left the glass in the sink and was going to clean it up after she got home from work (she left in a rush that morning).

Soooooo… here I am thinking I just took an L for my mom and I was just supposed to accept that? I for sure didn't want to be home anymore. I packed my backpack and I was going to leave. Didn't know where I was going to go, but I was going to go. Then I realized all I had in my backpack was some drawls, a few t-shirts and my favorite action figures. I couldn't take the Nintendo because I'd have to take the TV, plus I wouldn't have anywhere to plug it in. After thinking about all that I just sat in my room, looked at my bag packed that was clearly not going to leave the house, and I just cried. I got a weak ass apology and plus, my mom didn't get whooped for what was thought to be my fault and nothing could reverse that. I didn't want my mom to receive harm, nor any woman rather by any man, but that day I definitely gave it consideration as to what if.

Those kinds of whoopings brought tears of pain outside my eyes. Of course, the hits hurt (most of the time) but it was the pain that I felt that someone who was supposed to love me would cause me so much physical pain at the same time. That confused me a lot. Especially after I got a whooping and then my mom or dad would come and apologize for doing it and say they whooped me because they loved me. Like what? I'd wonder what you would do if you hated me! I just thought, if this is love I don't want it no more. The worst part I'd feel from that experience was taking a bath and just being in the restroom for a long time looking in the mirror and just fucking crying. That's something I don't advise anyone to do, its low key retarded and really odd that someone would stare at themselves crying. I don't know why I did it, but I just did. I'd wipe my eyes and another tear would just come down and I'd be like fuck! Then I'd cry some more. It was just terrible. I don't want you to feel that kind of pain. I want to do better as a parent. If you get out of line with enough reason where I know you know better and you chose to do bad, yeah, I'm going to be on your ass. But not just because I'm mad and I don't know how to express my frustration properly or I don't understand you the way you need me to. That's just not how I want to do things so this is my vow to you. I promise to listen. I promise to see your viewpoint and where you're coming from. I promise to be there for you. I promise to be a father first and a friend after. All I need is one promise from you... PLEASE, don't look at yourself crying in the mirror. I'm very serious. Save yourself!

Besides painful tears, there are such things as joyful tears. It might not be portrayed as much on TV, the media or even in songs, but it does happen. There are a lot of songs that describe crying with heartbreak when someone gets cheated on or left for someone else. That's typical too. I can just appreciate the songs that are about love and filled with joy for someone else because that's what I personally can relate to. Your mom is something special to me. She's an incredible woman with an incredible sense of understanding. It may not be right when you want it, but for the most part, it's there right on time. Her love is just different and it's crazy how things work. With all the things we've gone through together in what seems like a short period of time, it's enough to know that we have a deep love for one another. Some songs come on where couples sing together and say "Oh this is our song!" It used to seem corny until it happened to us. Daniel Caesar came out with a song called "Get You" and it was beautifully written by a homeless guy who happened to make a hit song about his feelings. This hit home because the situation and his words spoke so much truth in me and your mother's experience together. The first verse's lyrics read:

"Through drought and famine,
Natural disasters.
My baby has been around for me.
Kingdom's have fallen, angels be calling,
None of that could ever make me leave.
Every time I look into your eyes, I see it.
You're all I need.
Every time I get a bit inside, I feel it.
Oooooooooooooh.
Who would have thought I'd get you?"

These words meant so much because with us being together during the hurricane, her losing her favorite aunt, being homeless and hungry together, that's a strong kind of love to build on. I didn't realize that until later one day when we were in our apartment after all that happened. We bounced back together and it was cool because I felt any other woman would might have left me while I figured out how to get us back on top. We did it together and we did it not the normal way that you'd say "conventional" people would have done it. We did what was right for us. I was sitting at the table in the kitchen working on an art piece and your mom was in the living room working on hers. Next thing you know, the song comes on and I just start crying. Not like the sniffle wiffles either, I mean I just start silently balling hard than a bitch. She saw me in the kitchen crying and just walked over to me and asked what was wrong. I told her I didn't know, but I knew. That song hit so hard for me in that moment that I was just grateful for a love like hers to still be around and that's what brought those tears out. The fact that we had experienced so much before meeting each other, then having our own experience together in a way that some people wouldn't last, it was just crazy to me to still be blessed to have her in my life. It was those kinds of tears. No pain, no hurt, just love. I really hope you get the chance to experience that kind of joy through tears in your lifetime because it's a different kind of feeling I can guarantee you that. Love doesn't last always but when it's there and when it's good, it can be the best thing in your life if you let it be. Luckily, I found that in your mom. You are a product of that. I don't know how that makes you feel, but you should feel some kind of special because I don't care what no one says, you definitely are to me.

I've felt tears in another form of fear in a way I really hope you don't ever have to experience the way I have. Your teenage years are years you will probably remember for certain reasons. You may experience a lot of your firsts in those years. Your first bad grade, your first official girlfriend, your first heartbreak, maybe even your first drink of alcohol (if you're a rebel like your dad). For myself, it was a different particular end of my teenage years that made a difference for me going into my twenties. At age 19, I had experienced my first few close deaths of people close to me. My best friend, my favorite aunt and the only grandpa I knew most all had just died months after each other. I didn't know how to comprehend life and things just got confusing for me. I felt as if I was growing up fast yet wouldn't be given the opportunity to grow into my full potential. I wasn't as hopeful as I am today with what I was seeing around me and what I was reading as far as information about the world and its turmoil. I always heard that for the

Black youth, seeing the age of 25 in the United States was something that many wouldn't see. That was always a negative outlook to comprehend but seeing how some of my favorite music artists died before 25 and all my heroes I looked up to have been to jail at least once, I didn't see my future being as promising as I should have. Things became dark and for some odd reason I always had the numbers 22 and 78 repeated in my head and I thought that these numbers meant the ages of when I would die. I leaned more towards the age of 22 and that's how I felt for a long time in my early twenties. I tried to enjoy life as much as I could but when the age of 22 came for me, every day felt darker and darker. As I moved throughout the day, there would be like a dark shadow over my head and around me that would make me feel like death was near, very near. Every day when I was 22 was hopeless and I didn't know what to do.

Then one day, I saw death coming. I was driving on Hwy 290 and it had rained earlier that day. Going into Houston I was driving the speed limit in the fast lane. There was a car in front of me quite the distance away and I saw it push on the breaks where the back red lights came on and went off. I just left my foot off the gas a bit and stayed at a steady pace. Then the car pushed on the breaks twice and I thought nothing of it, but my car got closer and closer a bit faster than I expected.

Before my car could hit the back of the vehicle in front of me, I swerved to the right and there was a car I was about to hit beside me, then I swerved to the left and I was about to hit the side rail, I swerved to the right again to avoid that and my car did a whole 360 and a half. My car stopped in the middle of the freeway in the lane where my car was facing the direction of where I was coming from. In my lane coming towards my direction was an 18-wheeler and I couldn't start my car back up. After turning my key in the ignition and it not working, I just saw my life coming to an end and thought "This is it...fuck!" I turned the ignition twice... and nothing. One more time... (vroom) and my car started back up! I put the car into gear and drove quickly out of harm's way. I took the next exit into the Shell gas station parking lot and turned the car off. My hands were shaking on the steering wheel surprised I was really alive after almost dying back there. I just had my head on the wheel crying for like eleven whole minutes. Those tears were fearful tears because I just felt that was like a warning of some sort, yet at the same time a second chance.

Life can get really scary sometimes and negative outlooks can make things even worse. If I was mentally in a good position, I may have looked at that situation differently like a fluke, but that was definitely a sign or a reminder of something having to change. That something was me. I had to become more positive on life and appreciate it more. Life taught me a hard lesson and with continuing living, I've learned it's a lot more to learn and life is definitely not done with me yet.

Since you were born, I've been given the chance to have something better than just myself to live for, something to be hopeful for. Even with you here now, times can still seem weary. My problems over the years have gotten better for sure and I've learned to manage my feelings and even situations better now. With that, I still have a lot of improvement and my latest experiences have shown that to be true. In life, it's a blessing to have a good friend. One that you can call when times are hard and you need inspiration. Someone you can call to laugh about something you thought about that day. Even someone you can just pick up the phone to call and make sure that life is going well for them. Your uncle Kris is my best friend and although we aren't brothers by blood relation, he's just about as family as you can get with me. We've experienced college days together growing and learning about a lot and a friend like him is one you can really depend on. After you were born, I started working a new job at a call center where you dealt with customers and their insurance for their phones. People called about nonsense all the time and to be frank, I didn't want to be there. I just wanted to be home with you and your mom loving on all of y'all. I didn't want your mom to work especially after just giving birth to you so I had to make sure I was the man of the house and provided for you both comfortably. I didn't have a problem with that, I just really hated my job. It was consistently annoying, it wasn't difficult, just something I did to get easy quick money that was constant until our own businesses picked up the way we wanted it to. I'd get depressed the more and more I was there but I didn't want to give up because I had you all to provide for. I mostly didn't want to feel like a failure because I just thought that's what others may have thought I would be anyways. That was my first mistake, wondering what other people thought about me. But I needed help and didn't know what to do.

I started having negative thoughts like none before, suicidal thoughts. I didn't know why, but they would just come out of nowhere. I might have been at a stoplight and just thought, "I wonder if I run this red light, what would happen?" Right when I think that, a car comes from my left or right and I would think that I missed my opportunity. Shit was crazy and I needed to talk to someone. One day during lunch at work, I just left without any intention of going back, I called Kris and he was busy. I just kept driving. He called me back within 10 minutes because he felt he should. And for good reason, he was right. I told him how I felt about life and that I was just having a hard time wanting to provide so much and not feeling like I was at where I needed to be. He understood and gave me the right words of encouragement. He mainly also told me I needed to go back to work and that something was there for me. I didn't know and he didn't know but he knew I needed to keep going and provide for you because that's what a man does. I took his advice and went back to work.

I found out there was a mental therapist on site that the job provided so I made an appointment the next week. When I went to the therapist, I saw it was surprisingly a Black woman and I was glad. I would now have the chance to open up to someone who would professionally help me and understand (key things) my perspective and how I felt. The more we talked the more I opened up and realized the things that were bothering me. I cried a bit in the times I went to see her with the things I discussed. I was feeling unaccomplished and a failure because of certain things I've let change me in my decisions growing up with the parental guidance I had. The therapist allowed me the chance to see that I wasn't a failure after determining all the things I accomplished in just the year before that appointment. After that, I felt immediately different and that I've done a lot more than some could say they have in a longer time frame of life. I felt better about myself and I felt better about life. Most importantly, I felt better about being your dad. I wouldn't want you to feel like you haven't done enough in your life at whatever age, you can always keep going and you have until you die to accomplish what you set yourself out to do.

Make every day count and just know that you will always have loving parents in your corner to support you. Never feel that you can't count on us or even come to us to talk about anything. Even if you somehow do feel that way, make sure to go to Uncle Kris, he'll be sure to make sure you're on the right path of life to make the right decisions for you and what's meant for you. Those are the types of friends you need, no matter the kinds of emotions you feel, whether pain, sorrow, love, have the ones in your corner through it all to help guide you and let you know that you're never alone. You are loved and just know, it's okay to cry. Let it out. Those tears are reminders with each drop that you are still here, still able to make a difference, and still existing with a purpose to live out that is destined for you and you alone.

I'll Miss You Too

Now what I'm about to tell you may shock you. You may wonder what's going on and what to do, but don't worry. Truth is, I'm going to die. Not soon but one day I will. There's good news too though, you're going to die too. I know it doesn't seem like it's good news but it's the truth. It's one of the two things that's guaranteed in life, the other being living without knowing how long. Again, I don't want you to worry your sweet little head of yours, just know that while I'm here I am going to make the most out of our time together as memorable as can be. Although I'm away from you now writing this, I can't wait to hold you again. Being gone for half a year even has brought your mom to wonder how she would live without me around and raising you and your brother. I think about it too from time to time but I try not to as much because I am more hopeful of my lifespan living to see you become a man and all of that one day.

Death can be a sensitive subject I know, and it may very well come in different forms for many people. Some people get murdered. Some people die in accidents. Some people die from heart attacks. Most people don't know when or how they're going to die and I would believe that most people don't want to know. I think there could be a few ways I could see myself dying. None of them would be good because I'd probably still wish for another day with you all if I knew the next day was my last. Just don't worry about people telling you to move on and all that. Take the time you need to grieve, cry and let your emotions out. That's one thing I would need for you to do in the process of losing me. Use the power and strength of a loss as courage to move forward and keep going because you know that's what I would want you to do. Just make sure to ultimately do what's best for you every day. But whatever will happen, I just want you to be best prepared for it and have some kind of incite on what to do.

Now I may die from a bullet. As tragic as it sounds, who knows the situation of how it could happen. There's always the possibility I may be at a convenience store and it's getting robbed. I could be along with five other people and two of them are kids. The robber could have the gun pointed at a kid and I run in front of them before the bullet goes off. That would make me a hero of some sort. I can be in the woods and see a hunter at a short distance about to shoot a deer and I walk in front of the deer and take the shot to the chest. I'd still be a hero in a sense. I could even be in a hostage situation along side next to you. A gunman can give us two options, either you go or I go. I decide that your life is more important and choose to have the gunman take my life and they do. I might even then still be some kind of hero. I don't know why I'd prefer dying a hero when it comes to a bullet but I guess it would be more meaningful; way better than being at the wrong place at the wrong time.

If I had to die by bullet, I'd prefer the back of my head right behind the ear so that way the shot is instant and I don't have to sit and suffer in my own blood like they do in the movies. There's always this scene where someone gets shot and they say uncomplete sentences or things like "Tell my wife I said I love her and I'll always be…," or "Give this to my kid…". I just never want to live my last moment saying or doing the things I feel I should have been doing. So yeah, the bullet to the back of the head would be a solid choice my guy. Not speaking it into existence at all, but just know that's what I would have preferred. Now, you may feel resentment or anger of my death in this particular situation. I wouldn't want you to feel vengeful or feel like you need to get payback. Life will happen how it happens. On the contrary, I am hardheaded at times too so if you feel like you have to be an Avenger like a character out of Marvel because you can't let certain things go, I don't blame you. But I just want to give you a few tips, you know, just in case:

-take the body to a Louisiana swamp and feed to crocodiles

-dump body in tub of sulfuric acid,

-cut up body and melt to throw away in sewers

-pay a mortician to cremate the body for you

-put body in tank of piranhas

Don't ever say I didn't help with anything for you, do with this knowledge as you please, just keep it clean and on the low (Wink).

There is also a chance I may die by accident, and those tend to happen a lot. You haven't watched too much tv so far and who knows, you may miss out on generations of good movies to catch. You might not ever know about any of the Final Destination movies which are some of my favorite thrillers. It's basically a series of movies where a bunch of things happen in unbelievable ways where people die unexpectedly like a rollercoaster, a drive thru, construction, car crashes, a lot of ways! Those movies opened my eyes to the dangers of even the smallest things that could happen and its possibilities. I could very well try to scratch things early off my bucket list by trying to skydive on my day off and my parachute didn't work, how ironic would that be? I could even be driving and I get hit by a prison bus full of murderers, how ironic would that be? I might even be on vacation in October and trip and fall to my death, how ironic would that be?

Accidents happen and they can happen at any time, anyway. There is no way to avoid 100% accidents because that's what they are, occurrences that had no intention or knowledge of happening. If I so happen to get in a car accident, because I can see that more likely happening than anything previously mentioned, there are a few things I'd like you to do:

-check the body found in the crash (I have H-I-P-H-O-P tatted on my chest with a Houston H tat in the middle, if you don't see it then hold your tears, I faked my death and I'll be back soon to come get you)

-cancel the insurance policy we have on that vehicle (no need in continuously paying on something that was destroyed)

-grab the weed from the right hand side of the driver's seat (that's for you....shhhhh... don't tell mom)

Even if I do "die" from an accident, there may always be a chance of me coming back to find you. I might have gotten a real good lookalike and left it to burn in the car on purpose. I really might have faked my death and came up with a way to get that insurance money and escaped the country. You'll know by certain signs you'll see, or will you?

We of course can't ignore the idea that I may even die from health complications. Given the health of our family lineage on both me and your mom's side, there's:

-diabetes

-cancer

-stroke

-high blood pressure

-glaucoma

-and I'm sure there's more (but that's enough to get my point across)

One day I might just be at your football game cheering you on and next thing you know I'm looking like one of those guys on a Pepto Bismol commercial getting heartburn but it's really a heart attack and that's how I go out. That would be wild! But I'd hope your team would still win, even if you did have a loss with me. I do smoke tobacco from time to time and I've only been doing it for about twelve years now, which is pretty long enough. I'm learning my ways to get off of it like sticking to marijuana, which has no long-term effect on anyone as far as I know. I'm being hardheaded right now so just forgive me if lung cancer just happens to be the way out for me. I apologize. But I'll tell you what, if I do die by health complications, this is what I need for you to do:

-contact my lawyer and make sure your name is on my will (I want what I have going to you to go to you for sure, it's a MUST)

-go to the car and get that weed out from the right side of the driver's seat (I can't stress that enough!)

-drink as much water as you can, none of that Nestle shit either boy, I'm talking that alkaline water 7+ type stuff

-don't eat pork, if you're eating it now, throw that shit away!

-and wrap it up, especially if she's Spanish (not the Tupperware, I'm talking about your dick)

Of all the 1000 ways you could possibly die, if I could choose one, I would rather me die in my sleep. Just think about it. You already had a long day, you're tired and all you want is your comfortable bed. You lie down and snug yourself

161

in your sheets and blanket and fall gently asleep, only to never wake up from that good rest ever again. Would that be bad? I don't think so. That's how I truly wish to fly off this planet in this spaceship we call bodies. We go through so much in our lifetime and as humans we deserve peace. It seems like most of us get it the most when we are asleep, one with ourselves and away from the world.

You might be out all day, no, let's just say you're gone away from our home for years and you just wanted to say hello. You brought your love of your life home to meet your parents and you've waited for so long just to find a love like the kind your mother and I have. You finally wanted to prove to me that you found your success in the love you have. You all may come and visit us one day, and you kiss your mom on the cheek at the door. Then you ask, "Where's pops?" She replies, "Oh he must be in the room, go say hello." You come down the hallway walking like you're Vince McMahon down the ramp to the wrestling ring, you knock on the door and come into my bedroom... then you see me. My body lying in the bed, a smile on my face but not a movement in site. I'm not breathing. My body is cold. I'm gone, away forever. What do you do?

-remember that I fought the best fight every day

-keep in mind that I love you so much

-know that I did my best each day to be the best father I could be for you

-believe that I am in a happier place

-know that a piece of me is still living inside of you and you are not alone

-always remember, I'll miss you too.

Printed in Great Britain
by Amazon